Women Starting Over After 60

Inspiring Stories and Practical Tips

GiGi K

Table of Contents

Introduction

Starting over is a major life transition that can bring about a range of emotions and challenges. While some individuals look forward to an opportunity to pursue their passions, travel, and spend more time with loved ones, others may struggle to adjust. For those who have spent decades working and building a career, starting over can feel like the end of an era and a loss of identity. For others, it can feel like a brand-new chapter in life.

Author's Story

There was a time, back when I was a spry 50-year-old, weighing the option of ditching my daily grind to try my hand at being my own boss. My beacon of hope? None other than the poster boy of late bloomers, Colonel Sanders himself! The old man whipped up his first batch of finger-licking-good chicken when he was 65 and on social security. Why couldn't I create my own magic recipe too?

About that time, I met a retired bookkeeper at a nail salon—not exactly the place where you'd expect to get business inspiration. She'd taken up an art class, stumbled upon a secret talent for painting, and was now globe-trotting with her husband up and down the Californian coast, auctioning her pieces at art shows. Retirement plans? Not exactly, but they were loving the Bob Ross out of it!

Emboldened, I kissed my comfortable job goodbye and launched myself into the uncharted waters of being a virtual assistant. But alas, I was ahead of the times. Most people thought VA stood for Veterans Affairs or Virginia. A few understood and I did score some gigs, but not enough to keep the lights on.

This detour, however, did teach me that life is a lot like a GPS. It is always rerouting you when you least expect it. I dipped my toes into search engine optimization (SEO) since most people needed help getting their websites from the dusty back shelves of Google to the shiny glass showcase upfront. This newfound knowledge ended up being my golden ticket into new jobs focused on SEO for websites. But eventually, life spun the wheel again and I landed in client services, far from the world of SEO. This helped me realize my love for helping fellow business owners in a one-on-one setting.

Fast forward to the unwelcome guest of the century, Covid. It threatened to axe my job, so I took a quick detour into the world of notarization and loan signing. Luckily, I had my training wheels on before the job evaporated and I could kick off my mobile loan signing agent business. Did I mention this was during Covid? The interest rates were as low as my expectations for 2020. I was raking in decent money working part-time—the perfect setup for my 65th-year milestone.

However, good times are like houseguests—they don't last. My husband lost his job, we moved twice, the business revenue plunged, and the interest rates rocketed up. Pivot time was knocking again!

Now, at 68, I'm not exactly itching to rejoin the corporate rat race. But who's worried? Each pivot and each stumble has taught me that I can learn, adapt, and carve out new paths in life.

You won't find my name among the rich and famous, nor do I have a singular passion that consumes me. But my story is still worth telling. Like countless women who've made late-in-life career changes and have gone on to strike gold or fame, I have my tales to share. You'll find inspiring stories throughout this book.

This isn't a guide for the extraordinary but for the everyday person. Perhaps you're at life's crossroads, navigating a breakup or the loss of a partner, or maybe you're a retiree looking to supplement your income. I hope this book can shine a little light on your path.

Chapter 1:

Challenges of Starting Over

After 60

Case Study: Kathi

Balancing the responsibilities of two careers while bringing up five children, Kathi Muhammad was well-deserving of a relaxed life. But she chose a different path, transitioning into acting and initiating a charity.

Kathi Muhammad crossed the threshold of 60 a few years back, although she prefers not to specify how many. She says, "I don't see myself as that age. I feel more like I'm 40." Upon hitting the 60-year mark and stepping into retirement, she recognized it was the perfect opportunity to fulfill her dreams. "Delaying a dream or setting it aside for a while doesn't mean it should be forgotten," she emphasizes.

Muhammad had two long-standing dreams: initiating a charity and becoming an actor.

These ambitions would have appeared unlikely, perhaps even impossible, for much of her life. Muhammad's existence has been centered on accommodating others' needs: at home, as a mother to five kids she raised alongside her spouse; and professionally, in the U.S. Department of Defense, where she was "in charge of overseeing parking and construction projects, renovations, and HVAC systems." In her words, whenever a problem arose, she was the one to resolve it.

Even without considering her secondary job as a consultant for Mary Kay cosmetics, this routine seems incredibly draining. Yet, Muhammad always had a surplus of energy. "I eagerly anticipate each day. I always think: something new, something new. You can never predict what's going to transpire. I'm always ready to jump in."

Her initial endeavor was launching her non-profit organization, Serving Women Across Generations (SWAG), which organizes yearly panels and events for women in Prince George's County, Maryland, where she resides.

Never proclaim: I'm too old—I can't do this. Instead, always assert: This is what I aspire to do.

While serving as a federal police officer and later in the Department of Defense, Muhammad noticed her female-dominated workplaces were not very open. She says, "Many were reserved and withdrawn. In some families, it's a rule not to discuss what transpires within the family."

She was also initially reluctant to share. "I too didn't open up. My organization is founded on the belief that women need to communicate," she remarks. "We all face challenges and we all have solutions to those challenges. There's always someone else facing a similar situation and they can share their solutions."

Muhammad's parents, during her childhood, would often advocate: "Be responsible citizens. Give back." Her mother was a teacher and her father was employed by the transportation system in Washington, D.C. Taking their advice to heart, she volunteered at a children's library, assisted others in crossing roads safely as "a patrol girl," and served as a student counselor. "Whenever there was a need, I did my best to help. I firmly believe one person can make a difference," she asserts.

Upon Muhammad's 60th birthday, she believed she had arrived at the perfect moment to focus on her wishes. "Sixty gave me a sense of: How bad do you want to make this happen? Then do it."

She is constantly busy—she even continues to teach aqua cycling. Does she really think of herself as retired? "I'm retired from what I had to do and I'm not retired from what I want to do," she says. "I feel that now it is time to take care of Kathi. What does Kathi want? Because this is my life and I'm living it the best way I can."

When we read Muhammad's story, we can take a sense of hope from it. Societal norms are changing for us women over 60 and it is time to live the life you want.

How Did I Get Here?

Well, here I am, standing on the doorstep of my 60s, and it's not quite the doorstep I envisioned it would be. I thought by now I'd be sipping cocktails on a Caribbean beach, a best-selling mystery novel tucked into my beach bag. Turns out, reality has a sense of humor too, just like me.

Let's talk about retirement. Whoever came up with this idea must've been a fan of jokes, because there's nothing "retiring" about it. It's like life decided to throw me a surprise party I'm not ready for. I was all settled in my cozy little career, where the only decision I had to make was whether I wanted the corner office with the view of the parking lot, or the one next to the water cooler.

Now, I have the whole world before me and I'm supposed to figure out what to do with it? The irony is that my income has decided to take an early retirement, while I'm still showing up to the party.

Nowadays, I find myself spending more time looking at job listings than I ever did during my so-called "productive years." And believe me, navigating the modern job market is like trying to decipher hieroglyphics while blindfolded. One moment you're searching how to apply for a job online, the next you're trying to figure out why the webcam is showing your forehead during a Zoom interview. But, we're learning, aren't we?

Then there's the whole reevaluation of life goals. I mean, who would have thought that my passion for knitting miniature sweaters for my poodle, Sir Fluffington, could be a viable business idea?

Yes, life post-60 is a hoot! Suddenly, I'm attending entrepreneurial webinars, learning about e-commerce and getting an unexpected crash course in social media marketing. And to be honest, it's kind of thrilling. It's a whole new adventure, and I'm just getting started.

The point is, turning 60 isn't an end. It's a chance to reinvent yourself, to try new things, and to prove that age is just a number. If you find yourself needing to pivot post-retirement, just remember this—it's never too late to write a new chapter in your book. And while you're at it, make sure to sprinkle it with a healthy dose of humor, because as I'm learning, life doesn't stop being funny just because you've crossed the big 6-0.

Reinventing Yourself

Starting over after 60 might sound daunting. Many people see this phase of life as a time for leisure and relaxation, not as an opportunity for a new beginning. Yet, change is inevitable, and sometimes life forces us to reinvent ourselves, whether we want to or not. I have included some of the challenges you might face and how to cope with them.

Dealing With the Opinions of Friends and Family

Friends and family can be a tremendous source of support, but also criticism. When you decide to start over after 60, their opinions can add an extra layer of complexity to your decision-making process. Some might question your judgment, while others will encourage you.

Take, for example, my dear friend Maria. After she lost her husband to a sudden illness, she decided to sell her house and move closer to the sea, a dream they both had. Her two children were worried, reasoning that she was too frail to live alone, especially in a new town. She was faced with a difficult decision: Should she follow her dream or abide by her children's wishes?

What Maria did was communicate openly with her family, taking their concerns seriously but also emphasizing her own needs and desires. It took time and many conversations, but eventually, they understood her decision and supported it.

Remember that while it's essential to consider the thoughts and feelings of those who care about you, your decisions ultimately must align with your own desires and needs. Don't allow fear of others' opinions to hold you back from seeking your happiness.

Mental Mindset

The mental aspect of starting over can be the most challenging. Feelings of self-doubt, fear of the unknown, and worry about failing may arise. These emotions are natural, but they don't need to govern your actions.

Take Robert, a retired school teacher who always wanted to write a novel. At 65, he was battling against his inner critic, constantly telling him he was too old to start writing and would be unsuccessful. But Robert sought therapy, where he learned techniques to manage these negative thoughts and reframe them into positive affirmations.

Your mental mindset can be the key to your success or failure. You need to believe in yourself and your capabilities. Adopting a growth mindset, where challenges are seen as opportunities for growth rather than as obstacles, can be incredibly beneficial. Working with a counselor or coach can help you develop this mindset and provide you with strategies to overcome self-doubt.

Physical Issues

When it comes to the physical challenges of starting over in your sixties, these can vary greatly from person to person. Stamina might not be what it once was, or health issues could limit certain activities.

I have an acquaintance, Joan, who started her bakery at 62 and faced numerous physical challenges. Long hours on her feet, early mornings, and late nights were physically exhausting. She had to acknowledge her limitations and devise solutions that wouldn't compromise her health. Joan hired an assistant to help with the heavy lifting and took regular breaks during the day to rest.

Listening to your body is paramount. Ensure you maintain a balanced diet, regular exercise, and plenty of rest. You might need to be more strategic in your plans and be ready to delegate tasks if you need to.

Starting over at any age presents challenges. But the wealth of experience, knowledge, and resilience you've accumulated by your sixties can be an incredible asset. It's about balance: honoring your limitations while challenging yourself to step out of your comfort zone. You're never too old to begin anew, and every new journey can open doors to experiences that enrich your life.

Chapter 2:

Financial Constraints When Starting Over After 60

Case Study: Grace

After more than a decade in retirement, Grace decided to take on a new challenge in 2020, proving that it's never too late to pursue your dreams. As a postal worker for over 30 years, Grace spent countless hours at work, sacrificing time with her family to make ends meet. However, the physical toll of her job left her with continuous back pain and aches, leading her to worry about her health and financial future. Determined to secure a stable future for herself and her loved ones, Grace went back to school and earned her associate's degree in management and information technology in 2007. Despite facing challenges in finding steady work, she persevered and retired in 2008, hoping to pursue her passion for writing.

However, life had other plans for Grace when she and her husband purchased a house with their life's savings, leading to fears of losing their home with every mortgage payment. She realized she needed to go back to work and enrolled in the Senior Community Service Employment Program (SCSEP), a job training program for low-income adults that offers community service and work-based training opportunities authorized by the Older Americans Act. Through her determination and hard work, Grace was hired into a clerical job, providing stability and security for her family.

Specific Financial Obstacles

As a hilarious and gorgeous senior citizen, let me break this down for you in my own funny way. Here's the deal: Us wise owls, especially the ladies, make up a big chunk of the aging population. Why? Well, because we gals have a knack for outliving those guys! It's like a never-ending competition, but don't worry fellas, we still love you.

Now, here's where things get a little tricky. See, all this living longer comes with some serious financial risks for us senior ladies. We're more likely to run out of cash during our retirement years. And guess what? We didn't start off with a ton of money in the first place. But hold on, there's more! Do you know how life isn't always fair? Well, that unfairness follows us into the workforce. We get paid less, miss out on job perks, and end up with fewer gold-plated pensions. And guess what again? We often end up in the caregiving business, which doesn't exactly come with a fat paycheck or a pension.

We're juggling the financial burden of taking care of our loved ones, all while trying to make ends meet. It's like being a superhero on a tight budget. Not the easiest gig, I tell ya.

Oh, and here's the cherry on top: We're more likely to face health issues as we get older. Not only are we dealing with financial struggles, but we're also battling those annoying aches and pains. It's like life decided to play a mean prank on us.

In a nutshell, being an older woman isn't all bingo and shuffleboard. We face a whole bunch of challenges when it comes to money, work, and health. But hey, despite all that, we're still here, rocking those silver manes and cracking jokes along the way. Don't underestimate us!

When you are returning to the workplace or starting your own business after retirement, there is a lot that needs to be taken into consideration, such as:

Dealing With Financial Concerns

As a senior, I understand the financial struggles that can arise after reaching this stage of life. Let's review some issues and concerns we need to be mindful of.

Taxes

Taxes can significantly impact your finances during retirement or when starting over. It's important to be aware of the tax implications of different sources of income, such as withdrawals from retirement accounts, pension payments, and investment income. I highly recommend consulting with a tax professional who can help you optimize your tax strategy and minimize any unnecessary tax burdens. We need to be mindful of the following:

- **Limited retirement contributions:** Individuals who start a career later in life may have limited opportunities to contribute to retirement accounts like 401(k)s or IRAs. This means that they may have fewer chances to reduce their taxable income through retirement contributions.

- **Medicare premiums:** As people age, healthcare becomes increasingly important, and Medicare is a crucial part of that. However, Medicare premiums can increase significantly for individuals with higher incomes. Those who start a career after the age of 60 may see a substantial increase in their Medicare premiums, impacting their overall tax burden.

- **Social security taxes:** Social Security benefits can be taxed if an individual's income exceeds a certain threshold. Those who start a career later in life may not have as many years of contributions, which means that a higher proportion of their income may be subject to Social Security taxes.

- **Capital gains:** People who have accumulated assets, such as stocks or real estate, may face higher capital gains taxes if they sell those assets after starting a career later in life. This is because they may have held the assets for a longer period, which can lead to higher gains and thus higher taxes.

- **Required minimum distributions:** Individuals who have retirement accounts like 401(k)s or IRAs are required to take minimum distributions starting at age 72. These distributions can increase taxable income and potentially push someone into a higher tax bracket.

Inflation

Speaking as a beautiful senior, let me tell you, inflation is like my grandkid's growth spurt—it's the yearly hike in the price tag of pretty much everything. It's been bouncing around between 1% and 3% for a good while, but let me tell you, in 2021, it jumped like a cat on a hot tin roof (Stanley, 2022). Now, even if these percentages seem tiny, they slowly but surely eat away at your wallet's muscle. As the price of everything from bread to socks keeps climbing, folks are finding it harder to keep their heads above water, especially those bold souls who decide to swap their senior travel for briefcases later in life. And get this—lots of the stuff we golden-agers depend on are seeing their prices puffed up even more than average. Take health care costs, for instance. Even with Medicare Parts B and D and some extra insurance thrown in, we're still looking at coughing up a whopping $387,644 for the rest of our days, if you trust HealthView Services (Mercado, 2019). Now, isn't that a bitter pill to swallow?

It's important to have a diversified investment portfolio that includes assets that can keep pace with or outpace inflation. This may include investments in stocks, real estate, or other assets that historically have shown a potential for growth. Basically, don't put all your eggs in one basket.

Debt

Well, slap my knee and call me a senior! Here I am, cruising into the sunset of my years, and wouldn't you know it, a mountain of debt has decided to hop in for the ride. According to Mike Sullivan, a number cruncher over at Take Charge America, I've been too much of a softie, shelling out my hard-earned dough to help out the kids and grandkids. Now, don't get me wrong, it's a heartwarming business, being the family bank, but let me tell you, it isn't pretty when more than half of your wallet's drained!

Now that I'm living on a fixed income, it feels like I'm trying to pay my bills with bingo winnings. Life keeps dealing me wild cards—surprise medical bills, out-of-the-blue emergencies—and before you know it, my trusty old credit card is having a hotter workout than I've seen in years!

Here I am, retired but with a stack of IOUs higher than my favorite pile of detective novels. Between those ever-so-generous gifts to the kiddos and the not-so-friendly reminders from Mr. Mortgage and Miss Student Loan, I'm more a juggling act than a retiree. My bank statement reads more like a long-winded mystery novel where the plot's too thick to follow, and it's all too obvious that my fixed income is playing the invisible character.

Carrying debt after sixty can be a burden on your financial well-being. It's advisable to develop a plan to pay off high-interest debt, such as credit cards or personal loans, before retirement or beginning again. Reducing or eliminating debt can alleviate financial stress and free up more funds for your retirement needs. I mean, who doesn't want to get on the cruise to the Bahamas?

Social Security

The Social Security system serves many purposes, providing critical assistance to dependents of beneficiaries and surviving relatives of deceased employees, supplementing pre-retirement earnings for retired workers, and offering support for individuals with disabilities throughout the United States. As a major government initiative, Social Security plays a key role in the lives of more than 64 million Americans, serving as their primary source of income (Center on

Budget and Policy Priorities, 2020). The program is financed by a combination of government funds and the Social Security levy, which is deducted from your paycheck. Both you and your employer contribute 6.2% each, totaling 12.4%. If you are a sole proprietor, the entire 12.4% is your responsibility, though the "employer" share is deductible (IRS, 2019).

Social Security benefits can be a key source of income during retirement. However, claiming benefits at age 60 will result in a reduced monthly payment compared to waiting until you are fully retired. It's important to understand the implications of early or delayed Social Security claiming strategies and how they will affect your overall retirement income.

Well, now, sit for a spell while I give you the breakdown of this thingamajig they call Social Security benefits. If you've made it to my ripe age, and have your wits about you, you probably have a good grasp on the what's what.

See, here's the pickle—you hit 60, and you think you might fancy a bit of work to pass the time. Well, hold your horses, because this could lead to a kerfuffle with your benefits.

Let's say you're under the full retirement age (FRA, they call it, but it's nothing to do with a French airport, I assure you). That age, mind you, flip-flops depending on when you first started squalling in the delivery room. The more dollars you earn, the less your benefits might be. It's a bit like playing bingo with missing numbers!

And, heavens to Betsy, if you're raking in the dough while getting Social Security benefits, Uncle Sam may want a piece of that pie. Yep, that's right, taxes. And let's be honest, having your benefits taxed is like getting socks for Christmas—utterly disappointing! This could leave you with a slimmer check than you bargained for, and that could throw a monkey wrench in your financial hoedown.

Don't forget, when it comes to working and drawing Social Security, it's a tightrope walk. But hey, at least we're not juggling at the same time, right?

Medicare Coverage

As we get older, we may encounter increased healthcare costs that can put a strain on our finances. Even with health insurance, these expenses can add up and leave us with less money for other important things.

When someone turns 65, they are automatically enrolled in Medicare Part A, which provides hospital insurance and is usually free of charge. But that's not all: They also become eligible for Medicare Part B, which covers doctor and outpatient services, and Part D, which covers prescription drug costs. If they are already receiving Social Security benefits, the premiums for Part B and D will be deducted from their benefits check.

However, if you have applied for these benefits and have been receiving Part B coverage, withdrawing your application will have implications. You will still be billed for future premiums, and failure to pay them on time could put your coverage at risk of being removed. Therefore, it's essential to carefully consider the consequences before withdrawing your Social Security application if you are already receiving Medicare benefits. At the end of the day, you want to be prepared for every scenario.

Pensions

If you are fortunate enough to have a pension, it can provide a reliable source of income during your senior years. Understanding the terms and conditions of your pension, including any cost-of-living adjustments (COLAs) or survivor benefits, is important for financial planning purposes. You should also evaluate whether taking a lump-sum payout or annuity payment is the best option for your specific situation.

If you've previously received a pension from a former employer and are considering returning to work, it's important to be aware that your pension may be impacted. However, the specific rules regarding pensions may differ depending on the plan. If you decide to return to work for a different company, you may still be able to receive pension payments from your former employer while earning a salary from your new job, which can help increase your income stream. However, if you return to your former employer, your pension payments could potentially stop.

Navigating these financial struggles can be challenging, but with careful planning and professional guidance, you can make informed decisions to secure your financial future in retirement. Let's be honest for a quick moment. You have likely been organizing and managing the finances of yourself and your family for years. Look at it this way, now you only have to be concerned with yourself and how you want to live the rest of your amazing years.

I wanted to leave this chapter with some suggestions and advice I have learned personally along the way.

Well now, grab a chair and let me share a tale of how to navigate your golden years with a bit of spice and a whole lot of common sense. Let's talk dollars and cents, shall we? Before you start daydreaming about starting a new adventure, a new business, or just plain being an entrepreneur in your twilight years, take a good, hard look at your piggy bank. You must consider your incoming dough, your outgoing dough, your rainy day fund, and the money you've got growing in those investment pots. The bottom line is, you gotta be sure you've got the moolah to chase those dreams of yours.

Next up, I want you to try on a fancy little hat—your budgeting cap! This budget should outline your income, your expenses, and your financial aspirations. Don't forget to include any new costs associated with your new, shiny career or venture.

Now, here's a thought: Have you ever considered simplifying your life a little? If you're planning to embark on a new journey that may not fill your wallet as quickly as you're used to, how about cutting back on some luxuries? You might consider moving to a smaller nest, selling off some goodies you don't need, or just curtailing those non-essential expenditures.

Are you still feeling like a fish out of water when it comes to this money business? Well, here's a lifeline for you—a financial advisor. These money whizzes can guide you through the maze of investment strategies, retirement planning, and other money matters that can have you scratching your head in confusion.

A little apprehensive about your financial stability while starting anew? Well, consider moonlighting with a part-time gig or a side hustle. These can pad up your income while you're still busy putting your new career or business on the map.

Now, remember, life's full of surprises, and not all of them are as pleasant as finding an extra mint in your chocolate box. When you're starting over after 60, make sure you have a game plan for those unexpected expenses. An emergency fund or a contingency plan can be your safety net when life throws you a financial curveball.

It's never too late to start over; just keep your wits about you and remember to laugh along the way.

And so, dear reader, there you have it. Turning 60 didn't magically turn me into Warren Buffett. No, I had to wrangle with budgets tighter than my old school gym shorts and step around financial pitfalls that seemed to pop up more frequently than my grandchildren's birthday parties. I've had to pivot more times than a dizzy ballerina, and some of those turns were certainly a wild ride! But take it from me, this old dog has learned a few new tricks. I've found that while my body may grumble and groan, my spirit and my bank account don't have to. Financial constraints are just puzzles waiting to be solved. With the right approach, I've learned, they can become manageable. As I don my spectacles and peer at the fine print, I move forward with a gleam in my eye and a chuckle at the madness of it all. Life after 60, my friends, is an adventure. Bring it on, I say. My piggy bank and I are ready!

Chapter 3:

Rewards of Starting Over After 60

Case Study: Roslyn

Roslyn grew up in Bolton and London, where she left school at the age of 16. She went on to do a hotel reception course and worked as a secretary in an advertising agency. She later moved to southeast France with her younger daughter for love, and it was there that her interest in photography was awakened. After her partner's accident, she began to look through all the photographs she had taken and discovered her passion for patterns.

Despite not having any formal training in design, Roslyn's interest in patterns developed organically and gradually over the years. At the age of 60, she sold her first cushion on a market stall in southeast France, and it was the beginning of a new chapter in her life.

Roslyn's designs are inspired by the natural world and feature insects, flowers, and other elements from the environment around her. She puts her designs on various items, including cushions, lampshades, mugs, dress fabrics, and T-shirts that use British library images to celebrate black African hair. Her designs are unique and have gained popularity among customers who appreciate the attention to detail and the beautiful patterns.

Roslyn's journey to becoming a successful pattern designer is not only inspiring but also a reminder that it's never too late to pursue one's passion. She now sells her creations through her website and dreams of opening a little shop someday. Her new career has given her validation and fresh ambition, and she feels like a 20-year-old just starting out. Her journey serves as a reminder that following one's passion can bring fulfillment and a renewed sense of purpose.

A career change after retirement certainly seems challenging, especially after what we have discussed in the previous chapter. But if you have set out on the right path, you will be able to overcome those challenges with active participation. There's never a wrong time to embrace change. Your 60s and 70s present an exciting stage in life where everything around you is evolving, and you have the golden ticket to join the metamorphosis party!

Imagine you've worked tirelessly for decades, and finally, you've reached the golden years of retirement in your 60s. Now, you have the chance to kick back, relax, and sip margaritas on a beach without a care in the world. Or, perhaps you're the type who's planning for your family's future, diving deep into the exciting world

of life insurance policies, wills, and estate planning—
you can do it all!

The 3 Rs to Making Retirement Positive

I understand that retirement can be a major transition,
but there are multiple ways to make it positive and turn
it your way. Technically, there are three Rs to making
retirement positive.

Responsibilities

The responsibilities category encompasses a wide range
of tasks, operations, and duties that require our
attention. For those of us who work, our jobs are often
the most significant responsibility we have. However,
for retirees, this category can include a variety of other
activities, such as daily routines, hobbies, or caregiving.

Relationships

Relationships are the meaningful connections we
establish with the people in our lives. From spouses,
family members, and friends to social groups and
acquaintances, our relationships shape our experiences
and provide us with a sense of belonging. Whether they
are intimate, familial, or social in nature, nurturing our

relationships can have a significant impact on our well-being and quality of life.

Recreation

It includes everything apart from work that gives us joy. It can be a hobby, a source of entertainment, or even spending time with your loved ones.

The weightage given to each dimension of life varies from person to person and even changes over time. While some may prioritize work above all else, others may place more importance on relationships, leisure, or personal growth. Understanding how much each dimension means to us at present can help us determine how much time and energy we should allocate to it. Retirement provides an opportunity to adjust and reevaluate the importance we give to each dimension of life. Many soon-to-be retirees feel like they have not balanced these dimensions due to the dominance of work culture. Some may feel that they have not been able to devote enough time to their families or other interests due to work obligations.

While some may choose to focus solely on what they couldn't do during their working years, they may soon realize that they miss having a sense of responsibility or a challenge to complete. The three Rs can be helpful for them in giving them some sort of responsibility to feel completely satisfied. Even though they find something for only a few hours, it still allows them to make a contribution and give their life a sense of purpose. The three Rs make it easier for us to think about our needs and how we can address them.

A Sense of Purpose

Starting something new gives you a sense of purpose. Now, the definition of having a purpose can mean different things to different people. For some, it's the urge to give back to the community in any way. For others, it's doing whatever they can to make them believe in life. It doesn't always have to be world-changing either. It can just be a way to help your family or friends. It doesn't have to find the solution to world peace or cure fatal diseases, it can simply mean doing something that makes sense for you and working on things that express your unique skills to help others or contribute to a wider range of people.

A career transition can provide you with renewed purpose and motivation in your professional life. When you're feeling stuck or unfulfilled in your current career, a transition can be a game-changer, opening up new doors of opportunity and giving you the chance to pursue work that truly resonates with you. One of the unique benefits of a career transition is the opportunity to align your work with your personal values and goals. When you're doing work that feels meaningful to you and aligns with your passions, it can be incredibly rewarding, providing a sense of purpose and direction in your life.

Emerging research highlights the incredible benefits of living a life driven by a sense of purpose—where your actions align with your deepest values and aspirations. This purpose-driven lifestyle has been linked to numerous advantages for both physical and mental health, according to recent studies. One such study, which observed nearly 7,000 adults between the ages of 51 and 61, revealed that having a sense of purpose is linked to a lower risk of premature death. In fact, those who reported a lack of purpose were found to be almost twice as likely to die within four years of the study period (Gordon, 2019).

Beyond the potential for longer life, a sense of purpose has also been associated with promoting healthy behaviors and improving both physical and mental health outcomes. Researchers from the UK conducted a study in 2019 that found that a sense of purpose contributed to overall happiness and well-being for adults aged 50 to 90 (Steptoe & Fancourt, 2019). Additionally, recent research conducted with seniors in a retirement community suggests that a sense of purpose may have the power to alleviate loneliness (Brubaker, 2020). In other words, a purpose-driven life not only promotes better physical health but also contributes to greater emotional and social well-being, making it an essential component of a fulfilling life.

A New Array of Opportunities

Turning 60 is like getting a shiny, new "start over" button, and it's up to you whether you want to press it or not. Psychologically, after living a whole life, you're presented with a smorgasbord of options. Being 60 means you're like a wise old owl, with a lifetime of knowledge and skills to share with the next generation all around you.

Starting a career at 60 can be rewarding in so many ways. Let's look a little closer at them.

Personal Growth

Starting over after 60 is like embarking on a new adventure. A chance to explore uncharted territories and discover new facets of yourself. Just like a traveler who sets out to explore new destinations, starting over after 60 can allow you to broaden your horizons and develop new skills that you may not have even considered before.

It's like learning a new language, where you have to immerse yourself in a completely different culture and way of thinking. By taking up a new hobby or trying a different career path, you can challenge yourself to step outside of your comfort zone and try something new.

Moreover, starting over can be like hitting the reset button on your life—a chance to reassess your priorities and redefine what truly matters to you. It's like a second chance to create the life you've always wanted, but with the added wisdom and experience that comes with age. By reflecting on your past experiences and learning from them, you can gain a fresh perspective on life and create a more fulfilling and satisfying future for yourself.

Increased Confidence

Starting over after 60 can be like a superhero's journey, where you have to overcome obstacles and challenges to unlock your true potential. Just like a superhero who faces new foes and emerges victorious, starting over can provide you with the opportunity to overcome your fears and self-doubt, and emerge stronger and more confident than ever before.

This newfound confidence can spill over into other areas of your life, just like a superhero who gains a new level of confidence after defeating a villain. You'll feel more empowered to take on new challenges and pursue your dreams with renewed vigor and determination.

Mental Stimulation

Engaging in new activities can provide mental stimulation and help keep your brain healthy and active. Starting over can involve learning new skills, adapting to new environments, and meeting new people. These activities can provide your brain with the necessary stimulation it needs to stay sharp and healthy.

Research has shown that engaging in mentally stimulating activities can help stave off cognitive decline and reduce the risk of developing dementia or Alzheimer's disease (E. Budson, 2021). Starting over can provide a wealth of opportunities for mental stimulation, whether it's through learning a new language, taking up a musical instrument, or pursuing a new career path.

Better Social Network

The world of professional growth can be a complex maze, and often it's not just about what you know but who you know. A change of career can be an excellent way to break into new networks and expand your professional horizons. Not only does it bring new experiences, but it can also open doors to a wide range of new contacts that can help you grow and thrive in your career. Professional development activities, such as workshops, conferences, classes, and webinars, are all great ways to meet new people within your industry and make valuable connections. By connecting with new people, you can gain new perspectives, ideas, and insights that can help you grow and excel in your career. Moreover, making new connections can also help you stay up-to-date with industry trends and developments. It's like being a part of a dynamic and ever-evolving ecosystem, where you can stay ahead of the curve and make strategic decisions that drive your career forward.

Better Health

By adopting healthier habits and engaging in physical activities, you can shed your old self and become a new, healthier you. You'll feel more alive, more energetic, and more capable of taking on any challenge that comes your way. Whether you're picking up a new sport, starting a new exercise routine, or simply making healthier choices in your daily life, the benefits are clear. Visit a pickleball court—oh wait, this reminds me of a joke.

Why did the pickleball court start requiring an ID check?

Because there were so many seniors playing, they had to make sure they weren't mistaking it for the Fountain of Youth!

You'll improve your physical health, reduce your risk of chronic disease, and boost your overall quality of life. And who knows where that newfound vitality will take you? Maybe you'll finally take that dream vacation, start a new business venture, or pursue a long-held passion. The possibilities are endless when you're feeling your best.

Less Stress

Starting over can be a chance to let go of past regrets and focus on the future with a positive mindset. This can help reduce stress and promote emotional well-being.

For example, if you decide to leave a toxic relationship or a job that causes you stress and anxiety, starting over can be a chance to free yourself from the negative emotions associated with those situations. By focusing on the future and the opportunities that lie ahead, you can feel more optimistic and hopeful about your life.

Extra Income

Starting over can be a fresh start, a new beginning, a chance to create something truly special. By pursuing new financial opportunities, you can take control of your finances and achieve greater financial security. Perhaps you've always dreamed of starting your own business—now is the time to make it a reality. With careful planning and strategic decision-making, you can turn your passion into profit, generating new income streams and creating greater financial stability for yourself and your family.

Or maybe you're ready for a new career path, one that offers greater earning potential and greater job satisfaction. With the right skills and training, you can make a successful transition to a new field, opening up new doors of opportunity and setting yourself on the path to financial freedom. Starting over is also an opportunity to reassess your financial goals and priorities. By taking stock of your current financial situation, you can identify areas where you can make improvements and develop a plan to achieve your goals. With careful budgeting, smart investments, and strategic planning, you can build a solid financial foundation that will support you for years to come.

Greater Adaptability

Starting over can teach you to become more adaptable and resilient, essential skills in an ever-evolving world. When you start over, you are forced to adapt to new situations and challenges, which can help you develop the skills needed to navigate change.

For example, if you decide to move to a new city after 60, you may need to adapt to a new environment, a new culture, and new social norms. By embracing these changes and learning how to navigate them, you can become more adaptable and resilient, which can help you succeed in other areas of your life as well.

Inspiration for Others

There's nothing quite as inspiring as watching someone take a leap of faith and start over. It's a powerful reminder that change is possible, no matter what our age or circumstances. And when we share our own stories of courage and resilience, we can inspire others to take action in their own lives and pursue their own dreams. Starting a new business after 60 is a perfect example of this kind of courage. But if you succeed, you can inspire others to believe in themselves and pursue their own entrepreneurial dreams.

By sharing your story and your experiences, you can show others that anything is possible if you're willing to work hard and believe in yourself. You can offer practical advice and guidance, sharing your insights and lessons learned along the way. And you can serve as a role model for others, showing them that it's never too late to make a change and pursue your passions. But it's not just about starting a new business. Whatever your own personal journey may be, sharing it with others can be a powerful force for change. By being open and honest about your struggles and successes, you can help others see that change is possible—and that they too have the courage to pursue their dreams.

The Art of Giving Back

So far, we have discussed many of the rewards you get after retirement, but this one is by far the most precious for me. As you age, you get a lot of knowledge and wisdom and one of the greatest ways to share that wisdom is by giving back. As Winston Churchill said, "We make a living by what we get, but we make a life by what we give." Not only do you have the opportunity to give back to your community, but you also receive numerous benefits in return. Research has demonstrated the critical role that volunteering plays in maintaining the mental and physical well-being of older adults. Living a life of purpose and giving back can provide a sense of fulfillment and accomplishment at any age. Moreover, volunteering is linked to longer, healthier lives, as it promotes feelings of connection and purpose (Filges et al., 2020). It provides an opportunity to learn new skills, build meaningful relationships, and make a positive impact on society. From sharing your stories at a local soup kitchen to helping a student improve their reading skills, your age becomes an asset when helping others, adding a deeper sense of purpose to your life.

Let's look deeper into what giving back can give you.

A Chance to Connect

As we grow older, we may face feelings of loneliness or social isolation, particularly if we have lost a spouse or a close friend(s). Volunteering presents an opportunity for seniors to meet new people and engage in more active lifestyles. Even if it's challenging for you to leave your home, there are volunteer opportunities available where volunteers come to you. In assisted living communities, staff members organize volunteering opportunities for residents as well.

Recently, I had the pleasure of meeting a senior who volunteers her time to teach high school students how to enhance their painting skills. Being an artist herself, she shares her wealth of experience, including knowledge of painting techniques, art history, color theory, and suggestions on how students can showcase their art. Since she finds it challenging to leave her home, the students come to her for the lessons. She explains how volunteering to teach has given her something to look forward to, and an opportunity to get to know some incredibly talented students who share her passion for art.

Plethora of Health Benefits

As we age, we often find ourselves yearning to make a meaningful impact in the world. Volunteering not only has a positive impact on our communities and the nation as a whole, but it can also provide tremendous benefits to the individuals giving back and sharing their knowledge. Volunteering is an activity that not only keeps us moving physically but also mentally. Recent research has shown that people over the age of 60 who volunteer experience numerous health benefits, both physical and mental. Volunteers report better physical health than non-volunteers (Study: Volunteering Is Good for Your Health, 2020). Volunteering has been shown to reduce stress and increase positive, relaxed feelings by releasing dopamine—the feel-good chemical in our brains. Spending time in service to others can provide a sense of appreciation, which in turn can result in less stress. Less stress means a lower risk of many physical and mental health problems, including general illness, depression, anxiety, heart disease, and stroke.

An Opportunity to Enjoy Your Old Hobbies

Do you have an old hobby that you used to love, but haven't had the chance to pursue lately? Volunteering can provide the perfect opportunity to reignite that passion. By finding a volunteer activity that aligns with your interests, you can put your skills and knowledge to good use while engaging with something you enjoy.

For instance, if you were a teacher before retirement, you might enjoy volunteering at a youth center or school. If you love art, you could consider volunteering at a local museum or gallery. Similarly, if you have a passion for cooking, you could volunteer at a community kitchen. Volunteer opportunities exist in almost every area of interest, including building, business, and exercise. Don't be afraid to do some research and find a volunteer opportunity that best suits your interests.

Or Find New Ones

Do you ever feel like life has become too monotonous? If you're looking for a way to add some excitement and spice things up, volunteering may be just the solution you need. Volunteering provides countless opportunities to try new things and learn new skills that you may have never experienced before. If you're feeling stuck in a rut, consider looking for volunteer activities that are a bit outside your comfort zone. Whether it's teaching a new skill to others or working on a project that challenges your creativity, volunteering can help you discover an interest you never knew you had!

Starting over after 60 can be a rewarding experience filled with new opportunities and personal growth. While it may seem daunting to leave behind the familiar and venture into the unknown, the rewards of doing so can be life-changing. By starting over, you have the chance to pursue long-held dreams, try new things, and cultivate new relationships. You may discover hidden talents, passions, and strengths that you never knew existed. And, perhaps most importantly, you have the chance to reinvent yourself and create the life you truly want.

Of course, it has its challenges, but with the right mindset and support, you can navigate them and come out stronger on the other side. Whether you're looking to start a new career, move to a new city, or simply try something new, know that it's never too late to start over and create the life you want. Embrace this new chapter in your life and the possibilities it holds. It's never too late to start over and create the life you want.

Have you been thinking about volunteering but don't know where to start? Try https://www.volunteermatch.org/ You can explore volunteering opportunities in your area or just peruse the site to give you some areas to explore.

Chapter 4:

Understanding Your

Passions & Skills

Case Study: Betty

Hello there, folks! I'm Betty, a self-proclaimed master of laughter, and I'm here to share my uproarious tale of starting over after hitting the big 6-0. Life has a funny way of throwing curveballs, but I learned that it's never too late to embark on a new adventure and rediscover the things that truly make us tick. Grab a cup of tea and get ready to giggle as I recount my journey of identifying passions, pursuing sustainable activities, and embracing the laughter along the way.

After retiring from my decades-long career as an accountant, I found myself feeling a little lost, like a punch line without a joke. I decided it was high time to explore what truly brought me joy. I enrolled in a local improv comedy class. Stepping into that class, I felt a mix of excitement and nervousness, unsure if my timing would be as impeccable as it once was. Little did I know, this decision would unleash a tidal wave of laughter within me.

Improv comedy became more than just a hobby; it became my oxygen, the wind beneath my wings. I started performing at local comedy clubs, regaling audiences with tales of my newfound freedom and the quirks of aging. Laughter became my superpower, allowing me to connect with people of all ages. And the best part? It was a sustainable activity that kept me energized and purposeful.

While cracking jokes on stage was immensely satisfying, I soon realized I wanted to spread laughter beyond the confines of comedy clubs. That's when I stumbled upon a volunteering opportunity at a local retirement home. Armed with my sharp wit and a bunch of one-liners, I brought laughter to the residents' lives. Whether it was organizing comedy nights or leading joke-writing workshops, witnessing the joy on their faces made every punch line worth it.

But why limit me to just one avenue of laughter? I decided to explore new passions that made my heart skip a beat with laughter. I took up painting, and while my artwork was far from a masterpiece, the process of creating brought me joy. I even organized a humorous art exhibition, showcasing my whimsical masterpieces alongside hilarious anecdotes that had the audience in stitches.

As my journey continued, I realized that laughter had become more than just a personal pursuit—it had become my legacy. I started writing a memoir, recounting my hilarious adventures and sharing life lessons in a humorous manner. It became a joyful mission to bring smiles and laughter to others, especially those who needed it most. From book signings to speaking engagements, my goal was to inspire people to embrace their passions, no matter their age.

Starting over after 60 was the greatest comedy routine I never knew I needed. Through identifying my passions and pursuing activities, I discovered that life truly begins when you embrace the laughter within you. Whether it was making people laugh on stage, volunteering at a retirement home, exploring new hobbies, or leaving a legacy through my memoir, I learned that age is just a number when it comes to chasing your dreams. Let us all grab life by the punch line and keep the laughter alive, no matter what the calendar says!

Identifying Your Passions

Oh, let me tell you, friends! Discovering your passions after 60 is like finding a hidden treasure chest full of excitement and adventure. Now, I may be a divine and hilarious female over 60, but let me assure you, age is just a number when it comes to pursuing what sets your heart on fire. Here's my take on identifying passions at this wonderful stage of life.

First things first, my dear, let go of any preconceived notions about age limitations. Who says we can't try new things or fall in love with fresh hobbies? Certainly not me! Embrace your sense of curiosity and open-mindedness because the world is your oyster.

One way to identify your passions is to explore different activities. I'm not talking about the typical bingo nights or knitting circles (although those can be fun too). No, no! I mean venturing into uncharted territories. Maybe it's time to try salsa dancing, skydiving, or even learning to play the ukulele. The possibilities are endless!

Now, I must admit, some of these activities might be a little out of our comfort zone. But hey, that's where the magic happens, my friends! Break free from the shackles of routine and challenge yourself. You might surprise yourself with hidden talents or discover new interests you never knew existed.

Remember, it's never too late to pursue a long-forgotten passion. Did you once dream of becoming an artist, but life got in the way? Well, dust off those paintbrushes and create a masterpiece! Unleash your creativity and let it flow like a river of pure joy.

Another fantastic way to identify your passions is to spend time with like-minded people. Join clubs, organizations, or social groups that align with your interests. Surrounding yourself with people who share similar passions will not only inspire you but also provide a supportive community. And let's face it, having someone to laugh with as we stumble through new experiences makes the journey all the more enjoyable.

Always remember to embrace a sense of humor. Life is too short to take everything too seriously. Laugh at yourself, laugh at the mishaps, and laugh at the absurdity of it all. Laughter is not only good for the soul, but it also keeps us young at heart.

My fellow fabulous females over 60, let's go forth and explore, experiment, and embark on a passionate journey of self-discovery. Our age is just an invitation to live life to the fullest, to chase after what brings us immense joy, and to prove that passion knows no boundaries. Had I never taken the brave step of joining an improv group, I wouldn't be where I am today. That first leap of faith is all it takes to be on the path to a new beginning!

Now, if you'll excuse me, I'm off to learn how to ride a unicycle. Wish me luck!

Analyze Your Interests

Okay friends, listen up! Discovering your interests after 60 is a hoot and a half. I've had my fair share of adventures in the realm of discovering new hobbies and activities. Let's have a good laugh and dive into the art of interest analysis and exploring new passions in our golden years!

Remember that age is just a number, and you only have the limitations you put upon yourself. Now, where did I put my reading glasses? Ah, yes! Tips for analyzing your interests. This is all about introspection. Grab a cup of tea (or maybe a glass of wine) and get cozy. Start by asking yourself a few questions. What activities have always intrigued you but you never had the time for? What hobbies make your heart skip a beat? Is there something you've always wanted to try but put on hold due to family obligations or a busy career?

Once you have an inkling of your interests, it's time to explore, and trust me, exploration doesn't mean you have to sign up for bungee jumping or roller derby— unless you want to, in which case, go for it, you wild thing! No, no, exploring new interests can be as simple as dipping your toes in uncharted waters.

Tip Number One

Don't be afraid to start small. Take a class, join a club, or attend a workshop related to your newfound interest. If you've always wanted to paint, find a local art studio that offers beginner's classes. If you're curious about cooking, enroll in a cooking course where you can whip up delicious dishes while making new friends. Remember, laughter is the best seasoning!

Tip Number Two

Embrace the digital age! These days, the internet is a treasure trove of information, tutorials, and communities. Want to learn a musical instrument? There are countless online resources and video tutorials to help you strum your way to success. Enjoy writing? Start a blog and share your stories with the world. The online world is your oyster; just be sure not to get lost in a sea of cat videos!

Tip Number Three

Get out there and mingle! Join local community groups, attend events, and engage with like-minded individuals. You'll be surprised how many fascinating people you'll meet who share your interests. Plus, if you encounter any grumpy old souls along the way, well, just give 'em a wink and a smile. Life's too short to take things too seriously.

And finally, remember to approach your interests with a sense of humor and light-heartedness. Not everything will be a smashing success, and that's perfectly alright. Sometimes, the best memories are made from our little misadventures and blunders.

Let's embrace the joy of discovering our interests and exploring new passions. After all, we're never too old to have a laugh, try something new, and surprise ourselves. Happy adventuring!

Reflect on Things That Bring You Joy

Finding joy is a wonderful practice at any age. Let's explore some tips to help you cultivate that reflection:

- **Gratitude journaling:** Start a gratitude journal where you can write down things you are grateful for and that bring you joy. Each day, make it a habit to write down at least three things that made you happy or brought a sense of joy to your life. This practice helps you focus on the positive aspects of your day and cultivates a mindset of appreciation.

- **Surround yourself with positivity:** Surround yourself with people, environments, and activities that bring you joy. Spend time with loved ones who uplift your spirits, engage in hobbies or activities that you find fulfilling, and create a home environment that reflects your personal style and brings you comfort.

- **Mindfulness and meditation:** Incorporate mindfulness and meditation into your daily routine. Take a few minutes each day to sit quietly, breathe deeply, and focus on the present moment. This practice can help you become more aware of the simple joys in life and increase your overall sense of well-being.

- **Reflect on past experiences:** Take time to reflect on past experiences that have brought you joy. Reminisce about happy memories, achievements, or moments that made you feel fulfilled. Consider creating a scrapbook or photo album to preserve these memories and revisit them whenever you want to reflect on joyful moments.

- **Engage in self-care:** Prioritize self-care activities that bring you joy and promote your well-being. This can include activities such as taking leisurely walks, reading books that inspire you, indulging in hobbies you enjoy, or treating yourself to a spa day. Taking care of yourself physically, mentally, and emotionally will enhance your ability to find joy in everyday life.

- **Practice mindfulness in daily activities:** Bring mindfulness into your daily activities, such as cooking, gardening, or taking a bath. Pay attention to the sensory experiences involved, savoring the smells, tastes, textures, and sounds. By being fully present in these moments, you can cultivate a deeper appreciation for the joy they bring.

The key is to be intentional and present in your reflections. Take the time to slow down, appreciate the little things, and find joy in the simple pleasures of life.

Choose Activities That Are Viable

Being over 60 doesn't mean life slows down or loses its sparkle. Quite the contrary! It's a time when we can laugh a little louder, and enjoy life to the fullest. Now, when it comes to choosing viable activities, here are a few tips from this sassy lady:

- **Join a book club:** Let's face it, as women we rarely have time for doing things we enjoy. Oftentimes, we are overwhelmed with taking care of our families and working. If reading is something you love, why not engage in lively discussions with fellow book enthusiasts and explore various genres?

- **Volunteer for a cause:** We discussed the importance of volunteering for our health. Why not get involved in local charities, community centers, or nonprofit organizations that align with your interests and passions?

- **Take up gardening:** Cultivate your own garden or join a community gardening project to connect with nature and enjoy the therapeutic benefits of gardening.

- **Learn a musical instrument:** Pick up a guitar, piano, or any other instrument you've always wanted to learn. Take lessons or explore online tutorials to enhance your musical skills.

- **Engage in art and crafts:** Explore your creativity through activities like painting, pottery, knitting, or scrapbooking. Attend workshops or join art classes to learn new techniques.

- **Explore photography:** Invest in a good camera and capture beautiful moments from your daily life. Join photography clubs or online communities to share your work and learn from others.

- **Join a fitness class:** Participate in activities like yoga, Pilates, water aerobics, or dance classes specifically designed for older adults. It's a great way to stay active, improve flexibility, and meet like-minded individuals.

- **Travel and explore new places:** Plan trips to destinations you've always wanted to visit. Whether it's exploring local attractions or going on international adventures, traveling can bring new experiences and excitement to your life.

- **Engage in social clubs or groups:** Join social clubs, senior centers, or meetup groups that focus on shared interests such as hiking, cooking, or discussing current affairs. It's an excellent way to expand your social circle and engage in stimulating conversations.

- **Learn new skills online:** Take advantage of online platforms that offer a wide range of courses and tutorials. Learn a new language, explore history, enhance your cooking skills, or delve into any other subject that interests you. Please visit the resource page of this book to utilize the list of online platforms you can use to start your exploration.

The message here is you now have all the time in the world, so why not fill it with passions and interests you put on hold earlier in your life?

Now, why is choosing viable activities important? Well, staying active and engaged has numerous benefits for us folks over 60. First and foremost, it keeps our minds sharp and helps prevent cognitive decline. It also boosts our overall physical well-being, improving balance, flexibility, and strength.

Engaging in activities we enjoy also brings a sense of fulfillment and happiness. It helps ward off feelings of loneliness or boredom. Choosing viable activities not only keeps us physically and mentally fit, but it also adds a healthy dose of laughter and zest to our golden years.

Life is meant to be lived to its fullest, no matter how many candles are on your birthday cake. Go out there and embrace the world with a twinkle in your eye and a smile on your face!

Talk to Other Retirees

If you are sick, you see a doctor. If your tooth hurts, you see a dentist. At this stage, you are seeking wisdom and advice about life after 60, so why not chat with those who have been traveling this path?

Discussing this with people who are living it can provide you with real-life strategies, fantastic advice, and likely a laugh or two. Lean into those who have had their feet in the senior life pond for a beat. Listen to their stories, the good, the bad, and the ugly. You are likely to find inspiration here and you just may make a few new friends along the way.

Be Open to Experimenting

Let me tell you a little something about the importance of experimenting with new hobbies, interests, or activities after hitting the fabulous age of 60. Now, I may be a seasoned lady myself, but that doesn't mean I'm all dried up and ready for the rocking chair just yet. Oh no, there's still plenty of adventure left in these bones!

You see, life's like a big ol' buffet, and if you stick to the same old mashed potatoes and gravy, well, things can get pretty bland. But if you're willing to step out of your comfort zone and try new things, it's like adding a pinch of cayenne pepper to your plate. Suddenly, life gets a whole lot spicier!

Now, don't get me wrong, I'm not saying you have to go on an African safari or wrestle alligators. But trying out new hobbies or activities can be a real hoot. Maybe you've always wanted to learn how to line dance but never had the time. Well, now's the perfect opportunity to shimmy those hips and bring some sizzle to your life.

And let me tell you, there's no shortage of options out there, from painting to pottery, gardening to gourmet cooking, and it's never too late to try your hat at something exciting and new. Who knows, you might discover a hidden talent or passion you never knew existed. Maybe you'll become the next Picasso or the Julia Child of your neighborhood. Stranger things have happened, my friend!

Plus, trying new things keeps that beautiful brain of yours sharp as a tack. It's like giving it a little workout, flexing those neural muscles and keeping them on their toes. The next time you find yourself reaching for that same old knitting project or crossword puzzle, give your brain a challenge and pick up a guitar or a book on astronomy instead. You might just surprise yourself.

And let's not forget the social benefits. Trying new hobbies or activities opens up a whole new world of people to meet. You could join a hiking group, or even take up partner dancing. Trust me, there's nothing like twirling around a dance floor with a dashing partner to make you feel like a teenager again. Who says wrinkles can't have rhythm?

My wise friend, embrace the joy of experimenting with new hobbies, interests, and activities after 60. Life's too short to stick to the same old routine. Let's kick up our heels, try something new, and sprinkle a little laughter on this fabulous journey we call life.

Identifying Your Skills

As I approached my 60th year, I began to reflect on what I wanted my life to look like in the decades ahead. Suddenly, the idea of continuing in the same old routine seemed a little less appealing, a little less fulfilling. I decided it was time to find something new, to take the leap and embark on a second career, a fresh endeavor that could ignite my passions and utilize my unique skills. But how could I identify those skills, particularly ones I could use in this new chapter of my life? Here's the approach I took.

First, I took stock of my past. With so many years behind me, I realized that I had an extensive trove of experiences to explore. I started thinking back to my previous jobs and roles, whether they were in the professional realm or in my personal life. I noted down the tasks I excelled at and enjoyed, the activities that made me lose track of time, and the accomplishments that brought me the most satisfaction. Over the years, I have acquired a vast range of skills and knowledge that cannot be measured solely by degrees or certifications. It's important to recognize the value of this accumulated wisdom, as it forms the foundation upon which I can build my future endeavors.

Over cups of coffee in the quiet morning hours, I began to jot down these reflections in a notebook. This wasn't a simple list; it was a story, a collage of my professional and personal life that started to reveal patterns. The ability to plan and execute events from my days as a PTA member, the knack for resolving conflicts from my work in customer service, the joy and creativity of decorating my home for the holidays—these weren't just isolated incidents, they were threads in the tapestry of my life, highlighting skills and talents I may have overlooked.

Next, I sought feedback from others. I reached out to family, friends, and former colleagues, anyone who might have a unique perspective on my strengths and talents. I asked them what they thought I was good at, what they came to me for advice on, or what tasks they thought I excelled in. This outside perspective was illuminating, helping me see qualities in myself that I may have been too humble or too close to recognize.

In parallel, I also started exploring new interests and hobbies. As much as I cherished my past experiences, I also realized that I had an opportunity to try out new things. I took online courses, joined clubs, and even volunteered in my local community. This not only opened up new arenas of interest but also helped me discover previously unexplored skills. Who would have thought that my love for baking could translate into a proficiency for precision and patience, or that my interest in local history could denote a talent for research?

In this rapidly evolving world, I understand the significance of technological literacy. I assess my comfort level with modern tools and platforms, such as computers, the internet, and various software applications. If I find any gaps in my knowledge, I remind myself that it's never too late to learn. There are numerous resources available, both online and offline, that can help me enhance my digital skills.

Finally, I took everything I had learned about myself, and I started looking at potential careers where these skills could be utilized. There was a lot of research involved, and a lot of reading up on different industries, roles, and opportunities. I learned a lot in this process, both about the world and about myself. It was an enlightening, and sometimes challenging journey, but in the end, I was armed with the knowledge of my strengths and a vision for my future.

Starting over at 60 wasn't so much about starting from scratch as it was about building on a rich foundation of experience. By taking the time to reflect on my past, seeking input from others, exploring new interests, and mapping my skills to new opportunities, I was able to find a path that excited and fulfilled me. The road may be winding, and it may not be easy, but it's definitely worth the journey.

Improving Your Skill Set

I'm a proud, vibrant woman in her 60s and I am just getting started! My latest gig? You might call it "life reruns," only this time, I'm the writer, director, and star. My stage? The world! I'm embarking on a rollicking journey of self-discovery and re-invention, with a heaping spoonful of humor and a generous dash of sass. After years of dishing out life's assorted pies— cherry, apple, and occasionally, humble—I've decided it's high time I find out what else I can cook up. You know, that unexplored talent simmering on the back burner, just waiting to be served with a side of laughter. If you're looking for tips to discover your skill set, buckle up, buttercup! The hilarity, wisdom, and invaluable life lessons are just getting started.

Participating in Skill-Building Activities

Participating in skill-building activities can be incredibly beneficial for a woman over 60 who is starting over. Not only does it provide opportunities for personal growth and development, but it can also enhance self-confidence, expand social networks, and promote a sense of fulfillment. Let's look at some ways in which skill-building activities can be helpful:

- **Personal growth:** Engaging in skill-building activities allows you to acquire new knowledge and abilities, fostering personal growth. Whether you're learning a new language, developing artistic talents, or gaining computer skills, these activities can broaden your horizons and keep your mind sharp.

- **Boosting self-confidence:** Mastering a new skill or accomplishing a challenging task can significantly boost your self-confidence, self-esteem, and self-worth. It shows that age is not a barrier to learning and achieving, helping you to believe in your abilities and embrace new opportunities. You may feel more comfortable and valued as a contributing member of society.

- **Social engagement:** Participating in skill-building activities provides an excellent opportunity to meet new people and expand your social circle. Joining classes, workshops, or clubs centered around your chosen skill can connect you with like-minded individuals, fostering friendships and a sense of belonging.

- **Emotional well-being:** Starting over can be a challenging and emotionally demanding process. Engaging in skill-building activities can help you focus your energy on positive endeavors, diverting attention from any stress or uncertainty. It can also serve as a productive outlet for emotions, promoting overall emotional well-being.

If you are wondering how to get started, follow these steps:

- **Identify your interests:** Reflect on what interests you and what skills you'd like to develop. Consider hobbies you've always wanted to pursue or areas you'd like to learn more about. Choose something that genuinely excites you and aligns with your personal goals.

- **Research opportunities:** Look for local community centers, adult education programs, or online platforms that offer courses or workshops related to your chosen skill. Check out senior centers, colleges, or universities in your area that might offer relevant programs specifically tailored for older learners.

- **Set goals:** Define clear goals for what you want to achieve through your skill-building activities. Break them down into smaller, achievable milestones. Having specific targets can help you stay focused and motivated.

- **Take the first step:** Enroll in a class, sign up for an online course, or join a group or club related to your chosen skill. Don't be afraid to start as a beginner; everyone has to begin somewhere. Embrace the learning process and be open to acquiring new knowledge and experiences.

- **Practice and persist:** Consistency is key when developing a skill. Set aside dedicated time for practice and actively engage with the learning material or activities. Embrace challenges, learn from mistakes, and don't be discouraged by setbacks. Remember, progress takes time and effort.

- **Embrace a growth mindset:** Approach your skill-building activities with a growth mindset, believing that your abilities can be developed through dedication and hard work. Embrace the process of learning and enjoy the journey, rather than focusing solely on the end result.

It's never too late to embark on a journey of self-improvement. By engaging in skill-building activities, you can discover new passions, build confidence, and create a vibrant and fulfilling life for yourself.

As I reflect on the incredible journey of exploring new interests in my 60s, I am filled with a sense of fulfillment and wonder. I've learned that there is no expiration date on curiosity and personal growth. Embracing new hobbies, pursuing uncharted passions, and stepping outside of my comfort zone have breathed new life into my spirit, rekindling a flame of enthusiasm and vitality. Yet, I am acutely aware that embarking on this journey is not without its challenges. In the next chapter, we will look into the common barriers that may arise when starting over at 60. While the road may have its bumps, remember that with perseverance, resilience, and the wisdom that accompanies age, we can overcome any obstacle and continue to thrive. Together, let us unravel the secrets to triumph over these hurdles and unlock the next chapter of our remarkable lives.

Chapter 5:

Common Barriers to

Starting Over at 60

Case Study: Ethel

Hello there, my friends! I'm Ethel, a spunky 65-year-old lass with a twinkle in her eye, laughter lines to vouch for a life well-lived, and a quip at the ready for anyone who dares underestimate me because of my age or gender. Let me tell you a little something about starting over at 60. It's a wild ride, but there's nothing a few chuckles, a lot of grit, and a dash of tenacity can't overcome.

I want to talk about the big "A"–ageism. I remember when I decided to start my own knitting business at 60. Yes, you heard it right, knitting! My passion since I was a little girl. I went to the bank for a loan, and the young banker looked at me like I had three heads. He patted my hand and said, "Isn't this something you should have started 40 years ago, dear?" I looked him right in the eye and said, "Well, sir, I didn't realize knitting had an expiration date. Shall I send your grandma the memo?" He turned a lovely shade of crimson, but it didn't make the ageism sting any less. It was clear my age was a roadblock, not just in his eyes but also in the eyes of society.

Then there's sexism. You'd think we'd have moved past such archaic notions by now, but they are stubborn old coots, just like me! When I sought professional advice to scale my business, I was often overlooked or talked down to by the men in the room. Once, a young entrepreneur questioned if I understood "how business works"—in the middle of a workshop I'd paid good money for! So, I leaned over, adjusted my glasses, and said, "Son, I was managing budgets and balance sheets when you were still in diapers, so hush and let me get my money's worth!" Cue laughter from the rest of the room, and a newfound respect for my gumption.

Financial constraints were the cherry on top of this far-from-sweet cake. With my modest pension and limited savings, investing in my business felt like walking a tightrope. Marketing, supply chain, logistics, online platforms—each came with its own price tag, and it's not like money grows on trees. I had to get creative. I started using social media (after my grandkid showed me the ropes, bless her heart), started hosting knitting circles, and even struck a deal with a local cafe to display my creations. No one said it would be easy, and it sure as hell wasn't, but it was worth every penny-pinching, inventive moment.

The road to starting over at 60 is not without bumps, potholes, and the occasional fallen tree. Ageism, sexism, and financial constraints are all part and parcel of this journey. But let me tell you, there's something invigorating about proving naysayers wrong and demonstrating that passion and perseverance can't be constrained by your age or gender.

At the end of the day, my wrinkles are my badges of honor, my wisdom a weapon, and my humor a shield. If you ever find yourself at the precipice of a new beginning, just remember, you are capable. Now, if you'll excuse me, I have a knitting empire to build!

Ageism

I never thought I would reach this age and still be facing barriers to starting over. It's disheartening to realize that ageism is still a prevalent issue for women like me, who are over 60 and seeking a fresh start in life. Ageism is a societal bias that discriminates against individuals based on their age, and it affects women in particular, as we often face additional gender-related challenges (Loney, 2023).

First and foremost, the job market can be incredibly unforgiving to women over 60 who want to embark on a new career or find employment after retirement. Many employers, consciously or unconsciously, hold onto stereotypes that older individuals lack the necessary skills, adaptability, or energy to contribute effectively. This preconceived notion makes it exceedingly difficult to secure a job, even if we have the qualifications and experience.

Additionally, the rapid advancement of technology adds another layer of complexity. The digital era has transformed many industries, and those of us who didn't grow up with computers or smartphones may struggle to keep up with the ever-evolving technological landscape. This can lead to further exclusion, as employers often prioritize younger candidates who are presumed to be more tech-savvy.

Another barrier is the perception that older women should be content with their retirement years and not strive for personal or professional growth. Society tends to view us through a lens that suggests we should be winding down, enjoying our grandchildren, or focusing solely on our families. As a result, our aspirations and ambitions can be dismissed or belittled, making it challenging to gather support or encouragement from others.

Lastly, the pervasive ageist attitudes in society can affect our self-perception and confidence. When constantly bombarded with messages that we are "too old" or "past our prime," it's easy to internalize these beliefs and doubt our capabilities. This internalized ageism can become a psychological barrier, preventing us from taking risks or pursuing our dreams.

Despite these challenges, it's essential for women over 60 to challenge ageist stereotypes and pursue our goals. We have a wealth of wisdom, experience, and resilience that can greatly contribute to various domains. By advocating for ourselves, seeking out supportive communities, and continually learning and adapting, we can defy societal expectations and show that age should never be a barrier to starting over.

Sexism

As a woman over 60, I can certainly discuss how sexism often acts as a common barrier when it comes to starting over. Throughout my life, I have witnessed and experienced firsthand the pervasive influence of sexism in various aspects of society, and unfortunately, it doesn't disappear as we age. Let's look at some ways in which sexism can hinder women over 60 when they try to start over.

Stereotypes

As women, we face stereotypes most of our lives. Once we become senior women, this worsens. Some men believe we should always focus on our marriage over our careers. Some of our children will insist we spend these years focusing on them or our grandchildren. The corporate world has been known to scoff at the idea of women over 60 having value to contribute. Fighting through those stereotypes can form those solid boundaries you need to be successful.

Limited Opportunities

Sexism can restrict the opportunities available to women over 60. Some employers may hold biased assumptions about the capabilities of older women, assuming they lack technological skills, adaptability, or the energy required for certain roles. As a result, women may encounter difficulties finding employment or face limited career advancement prospects when starting over.

Wage Disparity

Sexism contributes to the wage disparity between men and women, which can be further exacerbated for older women. Women over 60 who decide to start over may face financial challenges due to lower lifetime earnings, fewer retirement savings, and inadequate pensions.

Lack of Support and Networks

Women often rely on support systems and networks to navigate professional and personal challenges. However, women over 60 may find it more challenging to build new networks when starting over, as many established networks may be geared toward younger individuals. Additionally, sexist attitudes may undermine the support that older women receive from friends, family, or colleagues, making it harder to pursue their goals.

Internalized Sexism

Over the years, women have been subjected to societal pressures and gender expectations that can lead to internalized sexism. Some women may have internalized beliefs that they are less valuable, less capable, or less deserving of opportunities as they age.

Overcoming these deeply ingrained beliefs can be a significant barrier when attempting to start over and pursue new paths.

Take me, for example. Growing up, my brother was often asked about his grades and his ambitions for college. I, of course, was expected to maintain good grades but my parents were more interested in making sure I knew how to cook and care for a family. My brother was never expected to help out with dishes because he had to focus on his future. It was never stated for a fact, but the presumption was there that I would finish high school, get married, and raise a family. My only expectation for the future was to take care of everyone else.

Despite these barriers, it is important for women over 60 to challenge and overcome sexism. Building a strong support network, seeking out mentorship opportunities, staying informed about current trends and technologies, and advocating for oneself are vital steps in breaking down these barriers. By asserting our value, skills, and experiences, we can challenge the limitations imposed by sexism and create new opportunities for ourselves, regardless of our age.

Financial Barriers

Well, honey, if I had a dollar for every time someone said it's difficult to start over at 60, I'd be sitting on a gold mine instead of talking about financial barriers!

But let me tell you, when you've got six decades of life under your belt, you've seen a thing or two. Most of the time, the bank balance doesn't reflect all that wisdom, unfortunately. It seems to have a preference for youth and recklessness.

The nitty-gritty is, we older ladies tend to face a few obstacles when we're trying to start afresh. For one, savings? Not as easy as it sounds. Let's not forget, many of us spent our prime years raising kids and looking after the home while our partners were out there earning. Not to mention, those years of free labor aren't particularly valued when it comes to Social Security or pensions.

And speaking of Social Security, it's a life-saver, yes, but also about as reliable as a pair of pantyhose. It's barely enough to cover the basics. Want to start a business or move to a new city? You might as well wish for George Clooney to be your next husband.

Then there's the pink tax. The pink tax is a term used to describe the tendency for products targeted at women to have higher prices compared to similar products targeted at men. This occurrence is often associated with gender-based price discrimination, as it is noted that many of the products subject to this phenomenon are colored pink (Fontinelle, 2021). Now don't get me started on this one. From health insurance to haircuts, it seems like they want to squeeze every last penny out of us. As if hot flashes weren't enough!

And ageism? It's as rampant as a teenager's hormones. Want to get a new job or a loan? Good luck with that!

It's almost like they see us as walking, talking antiques rather than capable, experienced individuals.

We've weathered our fair share of storms. This is just another to add to the list. After all, 60 is the new 40, right? And they say laughter is the best anti-aging cream!

Employment Barriers

Let me tell you, women over 60 trying to re-enter the workforce can face some real difficulties.

One of the barriers is the rapid pace of change in the job market. Technology has been advancing faster than a speeding bullet, and it can be a bit overwhelming to keep up. We may need a crash course in the latest software or a refresher on social media trends but don't count us out just yet. We're quick learners, and once we catch up, we'll be unstoppable.

Let's not forget about the good old gender bias. It's still alive and kicking, unfortunately. Some people might think that women over 60 are only good for gardening, baking cookies, or babysitting the grandkids. Well, guess what? We can do all those things and so much more. We've shattered glass ceilings before, and we're not afraid to break a few more.

Now, I don't want to sound all doom and gloom because there are employers out there who recognize the value we bring. They appreciate our work ethic, reliability, and the unique perspectives we offer. We just need more of them, darn it!

So, what's the solution? Well, companies need to embrace diversity and inclusivity, including age diversity. They need to realize that we're not looking for a retirement hobby; we still have a lot to offer and contribute. They should provide training opportunities and support to help us bridge any skill gaps. And let's not forget the power of networking and showcasing our talents. It's time for us to break down those barriers and show the world what we're made of.

In the meantime, we'll keep rocking our silver hair, sassy attitudes, and a killer sense of humor. Plus, who can resist the charm of a witty woman in her 60s?

Physical Barriers

Hold on, because I'm about to take you on a fascinating and hilarious tour of life north of 60.

The big 6-0 has come and gone, and what did I get? A party with an over-the-hill theme, a lot of "vintage" wine, and the desire to start over. But let me tell you, it isn't all fun and games. I mean, who thought it would be a brilliant idea to "reinvent myself" at an age when I can no longer read the tiny text on my phone without those glasses I keep losing?

First up, there's the fitness challenge. Sure, I used to be able to bench press my own weight, but these days, just the thought of doing so makes me want to take a nap. The spirit is willing, but the body... Well, the body's got about as much energy as a sloth after a Thanksgiving dinner. That doesn't mean I can't get fit, though! It just means my treadmill and I have a love-hate relationship. It loves to see me huffing and puffing, and I hate... Well, I hate it.

And let's not even talk about those yoga classes where I'm supposed to turn myself into a pretzel. The last time I tried, I was stuck in a position where even my cat gave me a look that clearly said, "Seriously?!" Still, I'm determined to conquer that Downward Dog, even if it means doing it my way, which is much closer to a "Lying Flat Cat."

Then there's the problem with my eyesight. Sure, it's not what it used to be, but on the bright side, I'm blissfully unaware of any new wrinkles or age spots that decide to join the party. The downside? Reading anything has become an adventure in creative interpretation, especially when I can't find my glasses. Those things have a mind of their own, I tell you!

But the most important barrier? Convincing myself that it's never too late to start over. Society might tell me I'm over the hill, but I'm still climbing mountains, even if it takes me a bit longer. There's something exciting about reinventing myself at this stage of life.

In a world obsessed with youth, I've got something far more valuable—experience and wisdom. I've faced challenges before, and I can do it again.

Well, well, well, ladies. It seems we've encountered quite a few roadblocks on our path to reinvention after 60. From society's insistence on putting us in a granny box to our own pesky self-doubt, it's clear that the world isn't always ready for our fabulousness. But fear not, for in the next chapter, we shall explore the magic of building a support system. Because let's face it, we may be sarcastic and funny, but even the wittiest among us need a helping hand now and then. Together we're going to shatter those barriers, embrace our inner reinvention queens, and build a network of support that will have the world wondering why it ever doubted us in the first place. Onward, ladies, because there's no limit to what we can achieve when we have each other's backs.

Chapter 6:

Building a Support System

Case Study: Irene

As a sweet woman in my sixties, I found myself at a crossroads. Life had presented its fair share of challenges, and I realized that in order to truly thrive, I needed to reinvent myself. However, I soon discovered that my transformation was not a solitary endeavor. It was through building a strong support system and finding a nurturing community that I was able to embark on a remarkable journey of self-discovery, reinvention, and personal growth.

Reaching out and connecting with others was a vital first step in my reinvention process. I actively sought out individuals who shared similar interests and aspirations, hoping to find like-minded souls who would understand and support my journey. I joined various community groups, enrolled in classes, and attended workshops tailored to individuals in my age group.

One particular turning point was when I discovered a local community center that offered a range of activities catering to the interests of older adults. From painting classes to gardening clubs, there was something for everyone. It was within this nurturing environment I met some incredible people who would become my pillars of support.

In this newfound community, I found a tribe of individuals who shared my desire for personal growth and reinvention. We formed deep connections, supporting and encouraging each other along the way. Regular meetups, sharing stories, and engaging in meaningful conversations became an essential part of our journey together.

With their unwavering support, I began exploring new hobbies and interests. Together, we learned to play musical instruments, mastered the art of meditation, and even formed a book club. The shared experiences and camaraderie helped rejuvenate my spirit.

Through the strength and support of my community, I felt empowered to revisit long-lost dreams and ambitions. One of my greatest passions had always been writing, but it had taken a backseat to the responsibilities of life. Encouraged by my newfound support system, I mustered the courage to pursue my dream of becoming a published author.

With the guidance and mentorship of seasoned writers within my community, I honed my skills and developed the confidence to share my stories. Through writing workshops, local literary events, and book clubs, I immersed myself in the world of literature, embracing my creativity and nurturing my love for storytelling.

The results were astounding. At the age of 63, I self-published my first book—a collection of heartfelt stories and life lessons. The outpouring of support from my community and the joy I derived from sharing my experiences with others was immeasurable. I realized that it was never too late to reinvent myself and pursue my passions with the unwavering support of those around me.

Building a Support System and Enjoying the Benefits

Reinventing yourself after 60 is like taking on a whole new adventure. And trust me, having a support system in place is absolutely vital. Now, why is it so important, you ask? Well, let me break it down for you.

To begin, as we age, we tend to have a few more bumps and bruises than we did in our younger years. And I don't just mean physically, although those creaky joints and achy muscles can be a real pain in the behind. I'm talking about the emotional and mental toll that life can take on us. Having a support system, whether it's family, friends, or even a group of like-minded individuals, can provide the encouragement and strength we need to keep pushing forward.

You see, when you're reinventing yourself, you're stepping into the unknown. It's like being in a pitch-black room and trying to find the light switch. Having someone there to lend a hand, or at least hand you a flashlight, can make all the difference. They can offer guidance, share their own experiences, and provide that much-needed perspective when you're feeling lost or uncertain.

Now, let's not forget about the power of laughter. As a woman with a great sense of humor, I know that life is a whole lot more enjoyable when you can find the funny side of things. And having a support system filled with people who can make you laugh, even in the toughest of times, can be a real blessing. Laughter can lift your spirits and help you navigate through any challenges that come your way.

Reinventing yourself after 60 often means stepping out of your comfort zone. It can be scary to try new things, explore different passions, or pursue dreams that have been tucked away for years. Having a support system cheering you on from the sidelines can provide the motivation and courage you need to take those leaps of faith. They can remind you that it's never too late to chase after your heart's desires.

Let's remember that having a support system can provide a sense of belonging and camaraderie. It's comforting to know that there are people who genuinely care about your well-being and are there to celebrate your successes and lend a helping hand when things get tough. They can offer a listening ear, a shoulder to lean on, and a safe space to share your hopes, fears, and aspirations.

If you're thinking about reinventing yourself after 60, I highly recommend building a strong support system. Surround yourself with people who uplift you, inspire you, and make you laugh until your sides ache. Together, you can conquer any challenges that come your way and create a vibrant, fulfilling life that's full of joy and adventure.

How to Find Your People and Build a Community

You're speaking my language now. Starting over at 60. First up, you gotta know who you are. What are you passionate about? What keeps you up at night, what gets you up in the morning? Is it skydiving? Cooking? Writing? Bird-watching? Dancing? Find what lights your fire and run with it.

Once you know what your passions are, go out there and find others who share them. There's a group for nearly every interest under the sun these days. Try local clubs, community centers, and online groups. And don't be shy to give something new a go! Who knows, you might find out you're the world's greatest salsa dancer at the ripe young age of 62!

Make sure you're open and approachable. You won't find your people if you're closed off. Smile, chat, and listen. You'd be surprised at how many people will be drawn to your energy. If you're genuine and kind, you'll attract the same.

Don't forget about volunteering, either. It's a fantastic way to meet like-minded people while giving back to the community. Whether it's at the local library, the food bank, or the animal shelter, there's always a need for a pair of helping hands.

And remember: Patience is key. Building a community takes time. It ain't gonna happen overnight, so give yourself some grace. Don't force it, just let it unfold naturally.

I wanted to add a short list of ideas on how to find your people to get you started.

- Every now and again, I enjoy attending religious services, whether in person or online. It's a fantastic opportunity to connect with like-minded individuals who share my faith or spirituality. Nowadays, many places of worship offer online options and discussion groups, making it even more accessible.

- Connecting with activity groups is another avenue I explore. There are numerous activity groups tailored for older adults seeking community and friendship. I check out community centers, churches, and senior centers in my area, and I also explore online options like AARP communities, Facebook Groups, or Meetup.com. Remember to utilize our resource page at the end of this book for more groups to reach out to.

- I also like to keep my brain sharp as a tack. Enrolling in continuing education courses is a great way to stay mentally engaged and forge connections. Whether it's academic classes like history or languages or more hands-on activities like music or sewing, these courses provide an opportunity to connect with fellow learners.

- I love to invite friends to join me for coffee or lunch, and I also accept invitations when they come my way. It's a give-and-take approach, and soon enough, my schedule is filled with moments spent with friends.

- Friendship and romance don't have an age limit. Read that again! I'm open to going on dates. Whether it's meeting someone in person or exploring online dating platforms, I embrace the opportunity to form meaningful connections and companionship. I mean, let's face it, we are hard-wired for physical touch and connection. There is no need to deprive yourself of this just because of your age.

- I find comfort and a sense of purpose in joining support groups. These groups provide a safe space for women like me to understand their feelings of loneliness and gain support from others facing the same challenges.

- From senior dance classes to walking clubs, water aerobics sessions to yoga meetups, I explore various options that I love and allow me to connect with more like-minded people.

- Striking up conversations with strangers can initially feel awkward, but asking questions can help break the ice. Whether it's in a coffee shop discussing their intriguing drink choice or inquiring about the book someone is reading, listening and sharing experiences can lead to new and exciting friendships.

- If you have the financial means, travel! See the world and meet new people. I love exploring our country because not only do I get to explore new places and cultures, but I also have the opportunity to meet fellow travelers and bond over our shared adventures.

- I also decided to get a part-time job because it helps me to continue to travel and pay the bills while also expanding my social circle. This part-time gig keeps my skills sharp, and I have made meaningful connections with like-minded beautiful women like me.

Getting back out there after 60 takes determination and patience. But is it worth it? Absolutely! Finding your tribe is just about connecting with the people who remind you of that, who make the ride a little more fun and a little less lonely.

Get out there and put yourself in the mix. Show the world what you've got. Find your tribe, build your community, and make the rest of your life the best of your life.

Don't forget—you've got this. Confidence is your best outfit. So wear it well, and strut your stuff. Starting over at 60 is nothing but a new adventure. So what are you waiting for? Let's get this party started!

Finding Mentorship and Guidance

Life after 60 doesn't have to mean settling down with a mug of herbal tea in front of the TV reruns. Oh no, it's all about reinvention, metamorphosis, and a touch of pizzazz! Here's the real lowdown on how you can find mentors and guidance to kick-start your new adventure:

- **Internet:** I used to think that surfing the web was a sport for youngsters, but here I am, advising you to do it too. There are online platforms, forums, and groups where you can connect with like-minded folks. LinkedIn is a goldmine, and Facebook has some fabulous groups. Start following folks who are reinventing themselves and you'll get lots of inspiration.

- **Book clubs**: Book clubs aren't just about books anymore. They're hotspots for networking and finding new friends. And you know what they say, one woman's memoir is another woman's guidebook! Some authors are great mentors, even if you never meet them.

- **Mentoring up:** Mentoring up is a concept that focuses on reverse mentoring, where younger individuals mentor older individuals. In the context of women over 60 starting a new career or business, mentoring up refers to the practice of younger professionals or individuals with expertise in a particular field providing guidance and support to older women who are embarking on a new professional journey. This mentoring relationship can be incredibly beneficial for women over 60 as they navigate the challenges and opportunities of starting a new career or business. Below are some ways in which mentoring up can be helpful:

o **Knowledge and skill development:** Younger mentors can share their expertise and provide guidance on the latest trends, technologies, and best practices in the industry. They can help women over 60 gain new knowledge and develop the skills necessary for their chosen career or business venture.

o **Networking and connections:** Mentors can help older women expand their professional network by introducing them to relevant contacts, networking events, and communities. This can open doors to new opportunities, collaborations, and partnerships.

o **Confidence building:** Starting a new career or business can be daunting, especially for women over 60 who may be entering unfamiliar territory. Mentors can provide support, encouragement, and motivation, helping to build confidence in their mentees. They can share their own experiences, successes, and challenges, providing valuable insights and reassurance.

o **Guidance on work-life balance:** Younger mentors can share strategies for managing work-life balance, which can be particularly important for women over 60 who may have additional responsibilities, such as caregiving or family obligations. They can provide advice on setting priorities, time management, and finding harmony between personal and professional life.

o **Personal growth and development:** Mentoring up can foster personal growth and development for women over 60. Mentors can challenge mentees to step out of their comfort zones, embrace new ideas, and pursue continuous learning. They can also offer guidance on goal setting, self-reflection, and resilience, helping older women to thrive in their new careers or business ventures. Mentoring up recognizes that age does not limit the ability to learn, adapt, and succeed. By leveraging the knowledge, skills, and fresh perspectives of younger mentors, women over 60 can embark on their new professional path with confidence, support, and the necessary tools for success.

- **Our peers:** Who says your mentor has to be a spring chicken or some hotshot executive? Some of my best guidance has come from my fellow golden girls. I believe that our peers can indeed be the unsung heroes in our search for a mentor. The wisdom, experience, and support they bring to the table can be invaluable as we navigate the challenges and uncertainties of entrepreneurship. One of the advantages of being in our age group is the wealth of life experiences we've accumulated over the years. Our peers have likely gone through similar journeys, faced various obstacles, and acquired a diverse range of skills. By tapping into this collective knowledge, we can learn from their successes and failures, gaining insights that can significantly benefit our own entrepreneurial endeavors. Peers who have already ventured into the business world can serve as mentors by sharing their practical advice, offering guidance on critical decisions, and providing emotional support. They may have encountered similar challenges or obstacles and can share strategies that have worked for them. Their firsthand experience can save us time, money, and unnecessary stress by helping us avoid common pitfalls. Additionally, our peers can offer a unique perspective specific to our age group. Starting a business later in life presents its own set of considerations and concerns. Peers who have faced similar circumstances can provide insights on managing these aspects while pursuing our entrepreneurial dreams. Moreover, our peers can also connect us with a broader network of contacts. They may have established relationships with other entrepreneurs, industry professionals, or potential clients that could be instrumental in growing our business. Networking within our age group can open doors to opportunities we might not have access to otherwise. Finding these unsung heroes among our peers requires actively seeking out individuals who share our entrepreneurial spirits and values.

- **Life coach or professional mentor:** Let's discuss these two options and how they can benefit you.

1. **Professional mentor:** But what exactly is a professional mentor? It is typically an experienced individual in your desired field who can guide and support you based on their expertise and personal experience. I have added some advantages of hiring a professional mentor:

    o **Industry insight:** A mentor can provide valuable insights into the industry you are entering. They can help you understand current trends, challenges, and opportunities, giving you a competitive edge.

o **Networking opportunities:** Mentors often have an extensive network of contacts that they can introduce you to. This can open doors to valuable connections, potential clients, and even partnership opportunities.

o **Skill development:** A mentor can help identify the skills you need to acquire or improve upon for your new career or business. They can guide you in setting goals, creating a development plan, and providing feedback on your progress.

o **Emotional support:** Transitioning into a new career or starting a business can be overwhelming. A mentor can offer emotional support, encouragement, and motivation, helping you navigate the challenges that come your way.

2. **Life coach:** A life coach is a professional who focuses on personal and professional development. They can help you clarify your goals, overcome obstacles, and create a roadmap for success. Below are some benefits of hiring a life coach:

o **Goal setting:** A life coach can assist you in setting clear, achievable goals aligned with your values and aspirations. They can help you break down big goals into smaller, manageable steps, ensuring steady progress.

- ○ **Accountability:** Accountability is crucial when embarking on a new career or business venture. A life coach can help you stay on track, providing structure, support, and regular check-ins to ensure you follow through with your plans.

- ○ **Self-discovery:** Starting a new chapter in life often involves self-reflection and self-discovery. A life coach can guide you through this process, helping you identify your strengths, values, and passions, and align them with your career or business goals.

- ○ **Confidence building:** Many individuals face self-doubt and fear when starting something new. A life coach can help you boost your confidence, develop a positive mindset, and overcome limiting beliefs, enabling you to take bold steps forward.

When deciding between a professional mentor and a life coach, consider your specific needs, preferences, and budget. Mentors are typically industry-focused and can offer specific guidance, while life coaches focus on holistic personal and professional development. Some individuals choose to work with both simultaneously, benefiting from the unique perspectives each provides.

If you're looking to reinvent your career, consider hiring a coach. These whippersnappers can provide targeted guidance and will make sure you're moving toward your goals at the pace of a greyhound, not a tortoise.

You know, reaching the golden years doesn't mean we stop dreaming, growing, or reinventing ourselves. In fact, it's the perfect time to shake things up and embark on new adventures. And what better way to navigate this exciting phase than with a community of like-minded individuals who appreciate the finer things in life, like a good chuckle and a shoulder to lean on?

Let's face it, life can throw some curveballs at us as we age. Sometimes it feels like we're juggling flaming torches while riding a unicycle, hoping not to fall flat on our faces. But that's where our support networks come in, those quirky, uplifting, and slightly offbeat bunch of folks who are there to catch us when we stumble and cheer us on when we soar.

And let me tell you, the jokes fly fast and furious. We've honed our comedic timing over the years, turning our wrinkles into punch lines and our gray hair into comedic gold. We find humor in the simplest things, like hunting for our misplaced purses or discovering new talents in the kitchen (who knew veggie burgers could be so delicious?).

In the end, it's the warmth and love we share with those around us. So, my friends, let's keep reinventing ourselves, building communities, and embracing the beauty of laughter, for it is the secret ingredient that keeps our hearts young, our spirits vibrant, and our souls forever ageless.

Chapter 7:

Creating a Plan

Case Study: Janet

Janet, a 62-year-old woman, lived in Boulder, Colorado. She had enjoyed a successful career as a dental hygienist, having retired five years prior. While she appreciated her free time in retirement, Janet soon found herself seeking more purpose and structure. She also noticed that her retirement savings were not stretching as far as she had expected.

Given her love for literature and her desire to stay active within her community, Janet decided to open an independent bookstore. However, she quickly realized that she had been out of the workforce for a while, and the landscape of running a business had significantly changed in that time. Furthermore, starting a business at her age presented unique challenges she hadn't faced in her teaching career. Nonetheless, she was motivated to make her vision a reality.

Janet sought advice from friends who were business owners and connected with local organizations. With this guidance, she quickly understood the importance of creating a solid business plan. She learned about market research, financial forecasting, marketing strategies, and operational plans—all integral parts of her business plan. This exercise helped her to critically assess her bookstore concept and strategize on the steps needed to achieve her goal.

Despite her passion and planning, Janet faced several speed bumps along the way. She realized the importance of understanding the latest technology for inventory management, social media for marketing, and online sales, and these areas she was not very familiar with. She also grappled with securing financing for her business as lenders were skeptical about lending to a new business owner at her age.

However, Janet didn't let these obstacles deter her. She enlisted the help of her tech-savvy grandchildren to get up to speed on technology. She attended workshops and webinars to learn about the best practices for social media marketing and e-commerce. For funding, she pitched her well-researched business plan to multiple lenders, participated in a local business pitching contest, and even launched a crowdfunding campaign, which garnered support from her community.

Janet's perseverance paid off. Within a year, she successfully opened "Janet's Literary Haven." It quickly became a cherished part of the community, providing not only books but also hosting reading clubs, author meet-and-greets, and children's story hours. The bookstore had a steady stream of revenue from both in-store sales and a thriving online platform.

Janet's journey of starting over later in life was challenging but immensely rewarding. She not only created a new source of income but also rediscovered her sense of purpose. She became a vital part of her community and learned new skills, keeping her mind sharp and active. Janet showed that it's never too late to start over and that age shouldn't be a barrier to pursuing one's dreams. In fact, her rich life experience and deep connections in the community became her unique strengths in her new venture.

Go For It!

Sixty and proud, I've been through it all—personal changes, societal changes, even technological changes. If you're asking me about starting over with a new career or a business, I say, why not?

To begin, we need to acknowledge the wisdom we've gathered over the years. We've been around the block a few times, have seen things, and have understood people and situations better. Doesn't that sound like the perfect recipe for an entrepreneur or a career changer?

Now, some folks may try to dissuade us, thinking we're too old to start something new, but let me tell you something. We've seen more sunrise and sunset than they have, and we've got the spirit to match! It's about time we took the reins and showed them what being over 60 truly means.

Be mindful that in this phase of our life, we're not starting from scratch, we're starting from experience. Whether it's a new career or a new business, we have a wealth of knowledge and skills that we've amassed over the years. That's our strength, our secret sauce.

Choosing to step into a new career or start a new business should be a decision of passion, not necessity. Find what makes your heart race, your mind curious, and your spirit soar. It will be your passion that proves you successful. For me, it's always been the challenge of doing something different, stepping outside my comfort zone.

It's not about competing with the younger generation; it's about complementing them. We have what they might lack—experience, wisdom, patience, and the ability to look at things from a broader perspective. We've got the spunk, the drive, and the gumption, and now, we have the time to focus and do something we truly love.

To my fellow women over 60 looking to start anew, I say, go for it! Don't let anyone define what you can and cannot do. Life is not about the number of years you've lived but about the experiences you've had and the ones still to come. Make the most of this time, and show the world that you're not just over 60; you're also over the moon with excitement for this new journey.

Launching a New Career

Who says that age has anything to do with ambition? If there's a fire in your belly, go ahead and stoke it. After 60, I've found there's plenty of time, freedom, and, frankly, wisdom to make the most of new opportunities. Let's get down to it.

Why a New Career?

The reasons why I would consider embarking on a new career after 60 can vary greatly. I might not be ready to retire and spend my days playing bingo; instead, I crave continued engagement and purpose. Financial considerations could also be a factor, but if my current career path feels stagnant and lacks passion, I might feel compelled to explore new avenues. I might sense that my skills are not being fully utilized and yearn to challenge myself further. Ultimately, the motivation behind starting a new career at this stage of life is deeply personal and individualistic. It's important to prioritize myself and make choices that align with my own well-being and the path I'm currently on.

Benefits of a Career Change After 60

There's no one better than me to give you the lowdown on this topic. Alright, pull up a chair, and let's talk turkey. I have included a list of the benefits for us lovely ladies of a certain age starting a new career:

- **New challenges:** Listen, we may have hit the big 6-0, but we're not ready for the scrap heap yet. Starting a new career shakes things up and keeps the ol' gray matter humming along nicely. Trust me, you'll feel more alive than you've felt in years.

- **Purpose and fulfillment:** I've heard some people say that after retirement, they feel somewhat adrift. Well, getting back in the game can give you a fresh sense of purpose, something to get you out of bed in the morning. And not just to make a cup of tea!

- **Financial independence:** You might think we've all got our nest eggs neatly tucked away by now. Well, you'd be surprised. A new career can provide some extra financial security and independence. It's never too late to add a few more feathers to that nest!

- **Pursuing passions:** All those years slogging away at a job that perhaps wasn't quite you. Now's the time to do something you're truly passionate about. There's something invigorating about turning a passion into a paycheck.

- **Social connections:** Starting a new career is a great way to meet new people and expand your social circle. A new job means new colleagues, new friends, and who knows what else!

- **Age as an asset:** We've been around the block a few times, and that's nothing to sniff at. With age comes plenty of life skills and experience. Don't ever let them tell you otherwise. You've got a lot to bring to the table, and a new career is a chance to show that off.

- **Inspiring others:** By jumping back into the workforce, you'll be an inspiration to others—showing them it's never too late to start anew. I mean, who wouldn't want to be a role model, right?

- **Personal growth:** New experiences bring personal growth, no matter your age. A new career can boost your confidence, increase your skills, and open up new horizons you've never dreamed of.

How to Change Your Career

I am here to remind you that there's no expiration date on chasing your dreams. Let's dive into the steps required to embark on this exciting journey:

- **Embrace your fabulousness:** You've got to believe in yourself. Recognize your strengths, experience, and wisdom that come with age. Embrace your fabulousness and let it shine!

- **Unleash your passion:** What exactly tickles your fancy? What makes your heart skip a beat? Is there a particular field or industry that's always piqued your interest? Follow your passion because when you love what you do, you'll never work a day in your life.

- **Research and network:** Once you've set your sights on a new career path, it's time to do some research. Dive into the nitty-gritty details of the industry you're interested in. Learn about the latest trends, skills, and qualifications required. And don't forget to network! Attend industry events, join online communities, and connect with people who can offer valuable insights and opportunities.

- **Fill the knowledge gap:** Now, let's be honest, the world keeps changing at lightning speed. If you need to update your skills or gain some new ones, go for it! Enroll in courses, attend workshops, or even consider online learning platforms. Learning is a lifelong journey, and age should never be a barrier to acquiring new knowledge.

- **Craft a fabulous resume:** Time to polish that resume! Highlight your relevant experience, skills, and achievements. But here's the cheeky part: Sprinkle it with a dash of personality. Let your prospective employers know that you're not just experienced, but also full of life!

- **Embrace the digital world:** In today's day and age, the digital realm is where the action happens. Make sure you're familiar with technology and the digital tools relevant to your new career. It's time to rock that smartphone, conquer social media, and show youngsters that you can slay the digital game too!

- **Be adaptable and open-minded:** Changing careers at any age requires flexibility. Keep an open mind and be willing to adapt to new challenges and opportunities. Life is an adventure—a flexible one.

- **Seek support and inspiration:** Surround yourself with a support system that uplifts and encourages you. Friends, family, and even like-minded individuals on the same journey can provide valuable advice and inspiration. Lean on those mentors. Share your goals and aspirations, and let their positivity fuel your determination.

- **Take the leap and enjoy the ride:** Finally, it's time to take the leap! Don't let fear hold you back. Embrace the uncertainty, trust in your abilities, and remember that this journey is all about discovering new horizons and finding joy in the process.

Now, go out there and show the world what you are made of. Chase your dreams with a sprinkle of humor and a twinkle in your eye. And always remember, life is too short to settle for anything less than extraordinary. Cheers to your fabulous new career!

Tips for Career Changes After 60

That's right, ladies and gents, this sassy senior is ready to tackle the world with a big smile and a mischievous twinkle in her eye. Now, let me tell you about two tips that are essential for this new chapter in our lives: staying fit and having a positive attitude.

Now, I know what you're thinking—*fit? At my age? Is she pulling my leg?* But trust me, it's never too late to get those muscles movin' and groovin'. Now, I'm not saying we need to become marathon runners or gym rats overnight (unless that's your thing, of course), but a little physical activity goes a long way.

You see, staying fit isn't just about looking good in those fabulous outfits we choose for our new careers. It's about keeping our bodies strong and healthy so that we can tackle any challenge that comes our way. Whether it's a demanding job, long hours, or even just keeping up with the younger crowd, having a fit body will give us the energy and stamina we need to excel.

Let's lace up those sneakers and hit the pavement for a brisk walk or join a fun exercise class tailored for our age group. And hey, who said exercise can't be fun? Dance your heart out, try out some yoga, or even pick up a sport you've always been curious about. The key is to find something you enjoy and make it a part of your routine.

When we talk about staying fit, we need to mention being mentally fit as well. Keeping our brains in top-notch working order is relevant when changing careers.

Let's move on to the second tip—having a positive attitude. Life is too short to dwell on the past or let negativity bring us down. We're starting our career over, which means embracing new opportunities and challenges with a smile on our faces.

A positive attitude is like a ray of sunshine in a world that can sometimes feel a bit gloomy. It not only affects how we perceive ourselves, but it also influences how others see us. Imagine walking into an interview or a new workplace with confidence, optimism, and a can-do spirit. People will be drawn to your magnetic energy, and doors will start opening left and right.

Sure, there will be setbacks and moments when we doubt ourselves, but that's just life, my friends. It's how we handle those moments that define us. So, let's remember to laugh at our mistakes, keep pushing forward, and never lose sight of our goals.

In conclusion, my fabulous fellow career starters, staying physically and mentally fit as well as maintaining a positive attitude are the secret ingredients to rocking this new chapter in our lives.

How to Start a Business

When I began researching this topic, I was immediately turned off. Why? Well, as usual, each link wanted to drag my vibrant, senior butt into the abyss of "old lady land." Oh, you want to start a new career after 60? How about teaching young ones how to knit or make preserves? That would be just lovely if I had ever picked up a knitting needle in my lifetime. I have also never made my own jam.

You will have to fight against society's expectations of what we should be doing with our lives at this age. You are strong enough to handle it. Fight against the suggestion that you work from home or enjoy this quiet time in your life. If you want to teach skydiving, then do that. If you want to become a travel vlogger, then do that.

Create a Business Plan

Here you are, a woman over 60 who's ready to take on the business world. I must say, that's a mighty fine idea! Now, let's get down to business and talk about creating a business plan.

Step 1: Idea Generation

To begin, we need a brilliant business idea. Time to put on your thinking cap and let those creative juices flow! Think about your passions, skills, and interests. Maybe you've always wanted to open a cat café where customers can sip tea and interact with kitties all day. Or perhaps you're a closet inventor and have a groundbreaking idea for a gadget that'll revolutionize the world. The sky's the limit, my friend!

Step 2: Market Research

Once you've got your grand idea, it's time to see if there's a market for it. I suggest starting with Google. It can be a great resource and there are plenty of websites to help guide you through the necessary steps of market research. Conduct your research to find out if there's a demand for your product or service. Look at trends, competitors, and customer preferences.

Step 3: Writing the Plan

Now comes the fun part—writing your business plan. This document will be your road map to success, so let's make it a good one. Start with an executive summary that grabs attention. Investors have a short attention span, so make it snappy! Then dive into the nitty-gritty details like your target market, marketing strategies, financial projections, and operational plans. But hey, don't get too carried away with jargon—keep it simple, like explaining business terms to your grandkids.

Step 4: Financial Shenanigans

Ah, the financials! It's time to put your math skills to the test. Calculate your startup costs, projected revenue, and expenses. Remember, we're not in our 20s anymore, so we've got to be a bit more conservative with our estimations. And don't forget to factor in the cost of extra caffeine to keep you awake during those late-night spreadsheet sessions!

Step 5: Making it Legal

No, no, I'm not suggesting anything shady here. We need to make sure our business is all nice and legal. Register your business, obtain the necessary permits and licenses, and don't forget about taxes.

Step 6: Marketing Magic

It's time to spread the word about your fabulous business. Get your creative juices flowing and come up with a marketing plan that'll knock everyone's socks off. Use social media, traditional advertising, and maybe even a catchy jingle to make your business unforgettable.

Step 7: Launching With a Bang

Finally, the big day has arrived—it's time to launch your business! Throw a grand opening party, invite your friends, family, and maybe even the local news. Make it a memorable event and show the world that age is not a barrier but a springboard. Oh, and don't forget the confetti cannons. Trust me, nothing says "business success" like a well-timed explosion of colorful paper!

There you have it, my adventurous entrepreneur, those are the steps to create your business plan.

How to Find Resources and Support

Now, let's talk about finding resources and support while embarking on this exciting journey. You will need help along the way, but so do all great entrepreneurs.

- **Connect with local organizations:** There are plenty of resources available to aspiring entrepreneurs, and many communities have organizations dedicated to supporting small businesses. Look for local chambers of commerce, business development centers, or entrepreneurship associations. These groups often offer workshops, mentoring programs, and networking events tailored to help you succeed.

- **Attend entrepreneurial events:** Don't be shy, my friend! Attend conferences, seminars, and workshops focused on entrepreneurship. These events provide an opportunity to learn from experts, gain valuable insights, and meet like-minded individuals who can become your support system. You might even discover potential business partners or investors who believe in your fabulous idea.

- **Seek out mentorship:** Find experienced individuals who have successfully started businesses and are willing to share their wisdom. They can guide you through the challenges you might face and offer valuable advice based on their own experiences. Look for mentorship programs through local business organizations or online platforms designed to connect mentors with mentees.

- **Leverage online resources:** The internet is a treasure trove of information and support. Join online communities, forums, or social media groups related to entrepreneurship, specifically targeting your industry. Engage in discussions, ask questions, and share your own experiences. You'll find a wealth of knowledge and a network of individuals who can offer guidance and support.

- **Explore government assistance programs:** Governments often provide support for small businesses through grants, loans, or subsidies. Research programs specific to your region and industry. Reach out to small business development centers or economic development agencies to learn about funding options and resources available to entrepreneurs like yourself.

- **Build a strong network:** Networking is key! Attend business events, join industry associations, and connect with professionals in your field. Build genuine relationships with other entrepreneurs, potential customers, and industry influencers. You never know who might be able to provide a helping hand, offer valuable connections, or become a loyal customer.

Starting a new business after 60 is an adventure worth embarking on. Embrace your enthusiasm, tap into available resources, and surround yourself with a support network that believes in your fabulousness. A small reminder of the resource section in this book to also offer some suggestions. Now get out there and move mountains and show the world what you are made of!

Overcome Barriers and Challenges

It's time for some wisdom and laughter from this fabulous woman over 60! Hold on tight, because we're about to dive into the wild and wonderful world of overcoming barriers and obstacles when women want to change careers or start a new business after 60. And trust me, darlings, if there's one thing I've learned in my time on this planet, it's that age means nothing when it comes to pursuing our dreams!

Let me tell you, I've had my fair share of obstacles in life. You, as a beautiful senior goddess, will also face obstacles and challenges while traveling this new road. Here are a few pearls of wisdom to help you navigate those bumpy roads when embarking on a new professional adventure:

- **Embrace your experience:** Don't ever underestimate the power of your experience. It's a treasure trove of knowledge that can be applied to any new career or business venture. Embrace it, flaunt it, and let it shine!

- **Surround yourself with cheerleaders:** We all need a supportive squad in life, especially when taking on new challenges. Find your people who believe in you and your dreams. These cheerleaders will be there to lift you up, encourage you, and remind you that age is just an accessory to your indomitable spirit.

- **Learn, learn, and learn some more:** The world is changing at lightning speed and it's vital to keep up with the times. Seek out learning opportunities, whether it's through online courses, workshops, or good old-fashioned books. Never stop feeding your curiosity and expanding your knowledge. Learning is a lifelong adventure.

- **Embrace the humor:** Life is a grand comedy, my friends, and it's essential to approach it with a healthy dose of humor. Laugh at your mistakes, find joy in the journey, and don't take yourself too seriously. Laughter is the elixir that keeps us young at heart and ready to conquer any obstacle that comes our way.

Age is often the excuse society throws at us. We have the power to redefine what it means to be a woman over 60, to chase our dreams, and to conquer new horizons. Embrace your fabulousness, keep your sense of humor intact, and let's show the world that there's no barrier too big, and no obstacle too daunting when it comes to pursuing our passions!

Now, who's ready to take on the world?

As I conclude this chapter, my heart is filled with excitement and anticipation for what lies ahead. It has been a joyous journey, navigating the possibilities and challenges that come with changing careers or starting a new business at the age of 60 and beyond. As a woman who values sweetness and humor, I firmly believe that laughter helps, and it has served me well in navigating the twists and turns of this path.

As we prepare to turn the page and embark on the next chapter of our lives, let us carry our dreams close to our hearts and wear our smiles as our secret weapons. Together, let's take bold steps, embrace the unknown, and bring forth the brilliance that lies within us. The world awaits, and we, the unstoppable women over 60, are ready to make our mark. Onward we go, with laughter as our guide and determination as our compass. Let's write the most extraordinary stories of our lives and inspire generations to come.

Chapter 8:

Taking Action & Moving

Forward

Case Study: Margaret

Margaret Peterson, a 63-year-old woman living in Austin, Texas, had spent most of her life dedicated to her career in secondary education as a high school science teacher. After retiring at 60, she quickly found the idleness unbearable. Margaret had always dreamed of opening a bakery and cafe, an idea born out of her passion for baking and her love for her community. At the age of 63, she decided it was time to reinvent herself and follow her passion.

Margaret began by drafting her business plan, defining clear and concise goals. She wanted to open a community-oriented bakery and cafe that would serve fresh, locally sourced pastries and coffee. Her goals included hiring local employees, especially those in need of second chances; using environmentally-friendly products; and giving back to the community by sponsoring local events.

She outlined a detailed business plan, which she reviewed and updated regularly. Margaret conducted extensive market research, understood her target customers, identified the unique selling points, projected financials, and planned the marketing strategy.

Margaret faced numerous struggles during her entrepreneurial journey, from the complexities of securing funding and understanding the regulations of the food industry to the practical difficulties of finding a suitable location and hiring the right staff. Being a woman over 60 also brought its own set of challenges, from age discrimination to physical stamina.

She had difficulties finding a bank that would provide a loan to a retiree with no prior business experience. Moreover, navigating the maze of food safety regulations and licenses was a formidable task.

Margaret worked tirelessly, often clocking in more than 70 hours per week, believing it was the only way to get her business off the ground. After six months of continuous hustle, she began to notice a significant decline in her health. She suffered from chronic fatigue, sleeplessness, and a lack of focus.

This was Margaret's wake-up call. She realized that she was burning out and her relentless work schedule was negatively affecting both her physical and mental health. It was at this point that she acknowledged the vital need for self-care.

Margaret began by taking small steps to improve her well-being. She started practicing yoga, prioritized sleep, and took out time every day for relaxation and mindfulness. She also outsourced and delegated tasks, an approach she initially resisted, but eventually came to terms with. This not only reduced her workload but also gave her the opportunity to employ and mentor others.

Margaret also sought professional help by visiting a therapist, who equipped her with the tools to better manage stress and maintain a healthy work-life balance. She took up hobbies that were unrelated to her business, such as painting and gardening, to take her mind off work and ignite her creativity.

After a year of dedication, persistence, and learning to balance work with self-care, Margaret successfully opened "Margaret's Muffins and More." The community warmly welcomed her bakery and cafe, and it quickly became a local favorite.

Margaret's story is a testament to the fact that it's never too late to follow your dreams. However, it also underlines the importance of self-care in the process. Without her realization and active steps toward better work-life balance, Margaret's dream could have turned into a nightmare. Today, Margaret stands as an inspiration not just to other aspiring entrepreneurs, but to everyone who wishes to reinvent themselves at any age.

Taking Action

Do you see that gorgeous woman over 60 with a sparkle in her eye and a spring in her step? That woman is me, and let me tell you, I'm ready to take on the world!

Now, some might say, "Why on earth would someone in their golden years embark on a new adventure like starting a business or changing careers?" And to them, I say, "Why the heck not?"

You see, life has a funny way of keeping us on our toes. Just when we think we've figured it all out, it throws a curveball our way. If I've learned anything in my six decades on this planet, it's that there's no better time than now to chase those dreams and make things happen.

But why push forward once our plans are created, you ask? Well, because the adventure doesn't end when the ink dries on our grand schemes. No, no, no! It's only the beginning. Starting a business or changing careers later in life is a testament to our resilience, our tenacity, and our thirst for growth.

You see, the world is constantly evolving, and we must evolve with it. We bring a unique perspective, an understanding of the ebbs and flows of life, and a depth of knowledge that is truly invaluable.

Sure, there may be challenges along the way. People may raise an eyebrow or question our choices. But you know what, my lovelies? We've weathered storms before, and we'll weather them again. Our age is not a limitation; it's a badge of honor.

So, let's push forward with all the fire and determination that resides within us. Let's prove that age is not a barrier to success. Let's show the world that there's no expiration date on ambition or reinvention.

And when we reach the finish line, let's not stop there. Let's continue to inspire, mentor, and uplift those who come after us. Because the true beauty of our journey lies not only in our personal achievements but also in the impact we have on others.

Let's embrace the adventure, forge new paths, and create a legacy that will be remembered long after we're gone. After all, life is far too short to sit on the sidelines. It's time to shine, to make a difference, and to keep pushing forward, no matter our age.

How to Set Achievable Goals

Starting a new career or business in our sixties requires setting achievable goals to be successful. I wanted to include some tips you should consider:

Set Realistic and Specific Goals

Break down your larger goal into smaller, more manageable tasks. Make sure your goals are specific, measurable, attainable, relevant, and time-bound (SMART goals). For example, if you're starting a new business, your goal could be to acquire your first ten customers within three months.

Prioritize Your Goals

The thought of starting a new business or career at this age might seem daunting to some. People often ask me, "Why not just enjoy your retirement?" But the fire in my heart simply won't let me sit still. I've learned that age is an advantage. The wisdom I've gained, the skills I've honed, and the courage I've cultivated over the years are all assets I bring to the table.

That being said, the thought of starting afresh does have its challenges. It requires planning and prioritization. Here's how I navigate my new ventures:

- **Reassess my skills:** I've learned a lot over the years, but it's important to understand what skills are transferable and relevant to my new venture. Maybe I need to brush up on some things or learn something entirely new. As I identify these gaps, I set out clear learning goals.

- **Set financial goals:** Starting a new business or career at this stage can be a financial risk. It's important to be clear about what you're willing to invest and how much you're willing to risk. Having a detailed business plan helps, but it also helps to consult with financial experts or those who've taken a similar path before.

- **Set personal goals:** At this age, it's easy to focus solely on business or career, forgetting that personal happiness and fulfillment are equally important. I ask myself, what do I want out of this venture? Is it just to keep myself busy, or is there a particular passion I want to pursue? Maybe there's a cause I want to support or a community I want to serve. Setting these goals helps me stay motivated and passionate.

- **Set health goals:** As much as I want to dive headfirst into my new venture, I also need to remember to take care of myself. This means setting goals for regular exercise, proper nutrition, enough sleep, and time for relaxation and socialization.

Determine which goals are most important to you and align with your overall vision. It's important to focus on a few key objectives at a time, rather than spreading yourself too thin. By prioritizing, you can direct your time and resources effectively.

Break Down Barriers and Overcome Age-Related Biases

I glance down at my hands; these hands that have seen six decades of life. I think about the countless experiences, obstacles, and triumphs they have assisted me through. The delicate wrinkles are a testament to my journey, and yet, I find myself at the dawn of a new chapter—starting a new business, diving headfirst into entrepreneurship. I am over 60, but I am not done. Far from it.

There's no denying that age-related biases are very real. There's this unfortunate societal tendency to see age as a decline, particularly when it comes to starting a new venture. As a woman of a certain age, the prejudices often double. They are compounded by both ageism and sexism. However, these biases have not deterred me. Rather, they've fueled my determination.

Let me tell you how I've managed to break down barriers and overcome these biases.

Embraced Change

We live in a digital era that changes by the hour and falling behind is not an option. I've made it a point to learn about the latest innovations relevant to my business. This includes utilizing social media for marketing, understanding data analysis for business growth, and integrating various productivity and management tools. It's been a steep learning curve, but a necessary one. It has also allowed me to relate to and connect with a younger audience.

Age as an Asset

Experience brings wisdom, foresight, and patience, which can often be a significant advantage in business. I've cultivated a narrative that highlights the value of my extensive life and professional experience. Age has given me resilience and an understanding of life. These are invaluable traits that I bring to the table as an entrepreneur.

Inclusive and Diverse Network

Networking is essential at any stage of one's career, and I've made sure to surround myself with people of different ages, backgrounds, and perspectives. This has not only provided me with valuable insights but has also challenged age-related stereotypes head-on.

Open and Clear Communication

By addressing age-related biases upfront, I've found that people often reassess their preconceptions. Honesty breeds respect and setting the tone from the start can prevent misunderstandings.

Every barrier is a challenge to be conquered. Every bias is a misconception to be corrected. So here I am, a woman over 60, shattering stereotypes and starting anew. Age will not define my dreams, my capability, or my worth. If anything, it enriches them. Starting a new business now is my testament to life's endless possibilities. To those who harbor age-related biases, I say, watch me. I am not just starting; I am thriving.

Continuously Learn and Adapt

I've been percolating on this planet for over six decades now, and let me tell you, there's not a wrinkle on my face that doesn't have a story or a laugh line that doesn't have a punch line. Now, I wanted to tell you about why it's so important to be a lifetime learner and be flexible when starting a new career or business venture, particularly for us ripe and ready ladies who've spun around the sun more than 60 times. So, here it goes.

I'd like to clear something up: When they said, "You can't teach an old dog new tricks," they were obviously talking about actual dogs. Humans are a completely different story. As for us, we have this delightful thing called neuroplasticity. It's like yoga for the brain and honey, my cerebellum can still touch its toes.

Why does it matter? Well, remember that time when your grandkid showed you how to video chat and you ended up accidentally snapping a selfie instead? You could have tossed your phone out the window in frustration, but instead, you persisted until you got the hang of it. That's what learning new things can do: It keeps your brain nimble and alert, and gives you an edge, especially when you're starting a new venture.

Starting a new career or a business at our age is like starting a new TV series—it's a commitment. It may take a little while to get into, but once you're hooked, oh boy! And let's not forget the look on people's faces when you tell them you just opened your own bakery or learned coding at 65. Priceless!

Plus, let's be honest, you've probably heard the phrase, "Variety is the spice of life." Well, when it comes to careers and business ventures, variety isn't just the spice; it's the whole darned recipe. Flexibility allows us to adapt to new situations and overcome challenges that come our way. It gives us the ability to change our strategies based on our circumstances. And let's face it, we've seen a lot of circumstances!

And in case you're worried about competition with those fresh-faced youngsters just out of college, just remember: We've got years of experience and a whole boatload of wisdom on our side. With that, who needs the stamina of a 20-year-old?

So, sure, you could rest on your laurels, become a professional couch potato, and watch the world go by. Or you can grab life by the horns, learn something new, take a leap of faith, and start that new venture. You never know where it may lead you. It could be the most fulfilling thing you've ever done.

Besides, as I always say, you're never too old to become younger. If you think I'm being facetious, I've got two words for you: bucket list. So, go ahead, learn that new skill, start that business, and take that risk. After all, who's got more moxie than us seasoned ladies?

And don't forget, as long as you're learning, you're not aging, you're just... marinating. Happy marinating, my friend.

Celebrate Milestones and Review Progress

Now, we're diving into the subject of celebrating milestones and regularly reviewing progress. Hold on because this is one ride you won't want to miss.

When it comes to starting a new career or business venture, numbers can suddenly become very important.

Oh, don't look at me like that—I'm not talking about the number on the bathroom scales or the number of candles on your last birthday cake. I'm talking about celebrating and regularly checking in on your progress.

You see, embarking on a new venture is a lot like going on a road trip. You wouldn't set out without a map, and you wouldn't drive for days on end without taking a break to stretch your legs, fill up the tank, and maybe even indulge in a slice of roadside diner pie. The same principles apply when starting something new. You need to map out your route (that's your business plan), and you need to take regular breaks to see how far you've come (that's reviewing your progress).

It's easy to get caught up in the nitty-gritty of daily operations and lose sight of the bigger picture. You might even start to question whether you're cut out for this new venture. Trust me, we've all been there. But taking the time to review your progress helps you see just how far you've come, and believe me, you've come further than you think.

And those milestones? Well, they're not just arbitrary goals or finish lines in a never-ending race. They're your roadside attractions, your points of interest. Celebrating them gives you a chance to take a breather, pat yourself on the back, and maybe do a little victory dance. Who cares if the cat's giving you a weird look? You've earned this.

In fact, celebrating your wins is just as important as learning from your mistakes. It's easy to be hard on ourselves when things don't go as planned. But remember, we're women over 60 and we've seen things, done things, and lived through things that would make a millennial's head spin. We've earned the right to celebrate our victories, no matter how small.

Whether you've just made your first sale, landed your first big client, or finally figured out how to make that blasted printer work, take a moment to revel in your success. Crack open a bottle of your favorite wine, call up your best friend, or even treat yourself to a well-deserved me day. Because remember, as we ladies of a certain age know, it's not just about the destination, it's about enjoying the journey.

Keep setting those goals, keep reviewing your progress, and above all, keep celebrating those milestones. They're not just marks on a chart; they're proof that you're moving forward, that you're learning, and that you're living. And isn't that what life's all about, no matter your age?

Take Care of Yourself

Well now, isn't this a topic that's right up my alley. Let's talk about the importance of self-care. This isn't like it was in your 20s, when you could burn the candle at both ends and still show up looking fresh as a daisy. No, we're playing a whole new game now, honey.

Let's start with the basics. Your health. That's the foundation of everything. You think you're invincible because you've made it this far. But trust me, your health isn't something to gamble with. You're going to need all the stamina, strength, and sanity you can muster. So, go get that checkup. Yes, the whole shebang. Eyes, ears, bones, heart, blood pressure, everything. Make sure you're starting on a good foot. Or two, preferably.

And for goodness sake, eat well. This is not the time to subsist on coffee and leftover pizza from the grandkids. Get some fruits and veggies in that belly. And no, potato chips don't count as a vegetable, however much you wish they did. Good nutrition is fuel for your body and your brain, and you'll need both working at top capacity.

Exercise? Yes, that's right, you're not getting out of that either. I'm not saying you need to be bench pressing twice your weight or running a marathon. I just need you to keep moving your body. It keeps the blood flowing and the joints flexible. Trust me, you'll thank yourself when you're darting around networking events like a spring chicken.

Sleep. Don't scoff. I know you think you can get by on four hours a night because you've "done it before." But you're not fooling anyone. You need your beauty sleep now more than ever. It's when your body and mind rejuvenate. And no, falling asleep in front of the TV with your glasses on doesn't count. Give yourself the gift of a good night's rest. And take a nap if you need to. You're the boss now, after all.

Don't forget your social life either. You may think you don't have time, what with your fancy new career and all. But you're a human, not a robot. And humans need connection, laughter, and yes, a good gossip now and then. It keeps the spirits high and the heart light.

Finally, keep that razor-sharp wit of yours honed. A sense of humor is like a Swiss army knife in the wilderness of life. It can cut through stress, tension, and all sorts of tough situations. Besides, who doesn't want a boss who can deliver a punch line?

There you have it, my pearls of wisdom. Remember, the best asset your new career or business has is you. Take care of yourself, and everything else will fall into place. Now, get out there and show them what a woman over 60 can do!

Tracking Progress

It's so wonderful to see women of our age taking on new adventures, whether it's starting a business or changing careers. It's never too late, is it? I would like to share some methods that I've found to be very effective for keeping track of progress when embarking on these sorts of journeys.

Set Clear Goals

One of the first things you should do is establish what it is you want to achieve. These could be short-term or long-term goals. It might be something like "Launch my website by the end of next month" or "Have 20 clients within a year." The important thing is that your goals should be realistic and achievable.

Create a Timeline

If you've decided to start a new career or business venture, let's get ready and set that timeline.

You might think setting goals is enough, and that'd be your first mistake. Goals are great—love 'em, couldn't live without 'em, but they're about as useful as a chocolate teapot if you don't lay out a plan to reach them.

After you've set your goals, we're going to make a timeline with milestones. Think of them as little signposts along the way, guiding you toward your grand ambition. Each one you cross off is a mini victory parade, a "huzzah!" moment, and a sign that you're one step closer to the finish line.

How do we go about this? Well, let's say you're opening a bakery, because who doesn't love fresh bread? First, you'll want to lay out all the bigger tasks you need to accomplish. Let's look at an example. "Marketing completed by April, grand opening scheduled for June."

Your goal is the grand opening in June. Great. How do we get there? Break it down like a funky beat on a Saturday night.

First, you need to finish your marketing plan by April. Within that, there are a bunch of smaller tasks. Maybe by the end of February, you need to have your logo and brand identity finalized. By mid-March, you've got to have your website up and running. By the end of March, you're aiming to launch your social media platforms. And by April, your marketing plan is all done, dusted, and ready to take the world by storm.

Then you move on to the next big thing: preparing for the grand opening in June. Maybe by the end of April, you need to have all the necessary permits and inspections done. By mid-May, you've got to have your staff hired and trained. By the end of May, you're aiming to have all your supplies and inventory ready. And voilà! By June, you're ready for the grand opening.

Starting a new career or business at any age can be a bit like wrangling a greased pig. But let me tell you, us women over 60? We've seen it all and we're not easily phased. So set those goals, lay out your timeline, and get ready to show the world just what you're capable of.

Keep a Journal

If you're considering keeping a journal to document your journey, I must say you're onto something marvelous!

As a woman over 60 with a sharp sense of humor (if I do say so myself), I wholeheartedly believe in the power of writing. There's something magical about putting pen to paper or tapping away on a keyboard. It's like capturing a snapshot of your thoughts, experiences, and emotions in real time.

You might be wondering, why bother with a journal when starting a new career or business venture? Well, my friend, let me tell you a few reasons why it's a splendid idea.

A journal allows you to note down your daily or weekly activities. Trust me, when you're embarking on a new adventure, things can get pretty hectic. By jotting down your activities, you create a record of your progress and accomplishments. It's like giving yourself a well-deserved pat on the back for a job well done.

But it's not just about celebrating the wins. Writing in your journal also gives you the opportunity to reflect on what worked and what didn't. As we say, hindsight is 20/20. By taking a step back and analyzing your experiences, you can uncover valuable insights. Maybe you'll discover a hidden pattern or realize that your gut instinct is worth listening to. Those "aha!" moments are priceless, my friend.

And let's not forget the lessons learned. Life has a sneaky way of changing the plot, especially when we're venturing into new territories. By recording the lessons learned in your journal, you create a personal guidebook for future reference. You'll have a collection of wisdom that you can revisit whenever you face challenges or need a boost of motivation. Think of it as your secret weapon, tucked away in the pages of your journal.

When it comes to the format of your journal, the choice is yours. Some of us are traditionalists and enjoy the feel of a pen gliding across paper. Others find solace in the digital realm, with apps and online platforms. Personally, I'm a fan of the good old pen and paper, but hey, times have changed, and we must adapt. Choose what feels most comfortable and enjoyable for you.

This new career or business venture is an exciting chapter in your life. And keeping a journal is like having a trusty sidekick on this wild ride. So go ahead, grab that pen or open that app, and let the words flow. Write about your triumphs and setbacks, your joys and frustrations.

And who knows? Maybe one day, you'll look back at your journal and realize that you not only created a thriving career or business but also crafted a masterpiece of your own story. Seize the opportunity, grab that journal, and let the adventure begin!

Utilize Technology

We might be in our sixties, but that doesn't mean we can't make the most of technology! There are so many applications and platforms out there that can help us monitor our progress, like project management tools and apps. Platforms like Trello, Asana, or Evernote can help keep you organized.

Regular Reviews

Setting aside a specific time each week or month to review your progress is invaluable. Reflect on what's going well and what needs improvement. Be honest and kind to yourself during these reviews. Change is a process and it's okay to make mistakes as long as you learn from them.

Network and Get Feedback

Connect with others in your industry. This not only opens up opportunities for collaboration and learning but it also gives you a chance to get feedback on your progress. This can be particularly useful in getting an external perspective and maybe spotting something you've missed.

Celebrate Your Wins

This is something women often forget to do, but it's so important! Recognize your victories, big and small, and take time to celebrate them. This helps boost your morale and keeps the journey enjoyable. I would go so far as to say, celebrate every last one of them. Your first paying customer could equal a celebratory lunch. Your 50th paying customer could amount to a spa day.

Changing careers or starting a business, especially at our age, can be a lot. But with patience, persistence, and a bit of organization, we can certainly make it a successful one. Most importantly, enjoy the process. It's all about growth and learning, and we've got plenty of that ahead of us!

Self-Care

It was recently pointed out to me how I have not been taking care of myself. This is a close personal friend and

I cherish their presence in my life. We have known each other for more than thirty years, so if anyone could tell I am worn out, it would be her. At her suggestion, I recently visited a therapist. Her suggestions are mirrored in my advice below.

I wanted to create a dedicated space that you can refer back to whenever necessary. This space is a sanctuary where you can find solace without any judgment, advice, or suggestions.

Here, you can retreat during moments when you need an extra source of encouragement. It serves as a reminder of how extraordinary and remarkable you truly are.

Are you feeling overwhelmed by negative comments? Are you tired of hearing that you're "too old" for certain things? Perhaps you're ready to dismiss those who suggest you should simply relax and enjoy the final phase of your journey. And can we take a moment and discuss one of our biggest obstacles, our own negative self-talk? Yes, it is true, you will get plenty of advice from those who have no skin in the game, but how you talk to yourself is important. We have all been there. The tape begins to play like a movie in your head and the negativity and anxious thoughts begin. *What if I lose everything I have? What if I fail? If I do this and it flops, I will have no savings for retirement.* On and on it goes until we convince ourselves to back out.

When you no longer want to deal with negativity or insulting remarks, this is the place you can turn to. This space exists to help you remember your uniqueness. You are diligent, devoted, and passionate. You deserve recognition and support. You deserve encouragement and love. You can come here to find all of that.

Visit this space for gentle reminders about self-care. Despite the busyness of carving new paths in this world, it's vital to stay energized and well-rested. At our age, burnout, exhaustion, and feeling overwhelmed can come more easily, so being mindful of this is a good starting point. Knowing your limits and understanding what rejuvenates you is essential.

Come here to remind yourself of your "why." On those days when even getting out of bed seems challenging, remember why you're doing this. Recall all the incredible things it brings to your life and the legacy you're creating.

Be kind to yourself, especially on the tough days. Be proud of yourself every single day. Remain curious and continue to educate and empower yourself. Show courage and bravery as you demonstrate to the younger generation of women how powerful we truly are.

You are loved, supported, and admired. Keep embracing your incredible self!

Whether you're reentering the job market or planning to start your own business, here are some self-care tips that I swear by.

- **Meditate and relax:** It's about keeping your mind sharp and your body strong. Find a routine you enjoy and stick to it. Our brains might feel like a 20-year-olds, but remember, we still need to relax!

- **Proper nutrition is key:** Feed your body and mind with nourishing food. You'd be surprised how much better you feel when you take care of yourself from the inside out. A balanced diet rich in fruits, vegetables, lean protein, and whole grains will do you wonders.

- **Dress in confidence:** Style doesn't have an age limit, and feeling good in your clothes can be a major confidence booster. Choose pieces that make you feel vibrant, powerful, and stylish. And remember, comfort is king. High heels may look good, but flats won't give you blisters. Prioritize your comfort and hey, who doesn't love a good shopping trip to give back to ourselves?

- **Mind your mental health:** Just as it's important to care for your physical health, pay attention to your mental well-being. If you feel overwhelmed, stressed, or anxious, don't hesitate to seek support. Therapy is not a dirty word, love; it's self-care.

- **Find time for hobbies:** Work is important, but so is play. Keep up with your interests and hobbies. They provide a creative outlet, relieve stress, and just add a little bit of sparkle to life.

- **Listen to your body:** If you're feeling tired or rundown, give yourself permission to rest. It's not a sign of weakness; it's a signal that your body needs to recharge. We aren't machines, after all.

- **Preventative care:** Keep up with regular medical check-ups. This includes annual physicals, eye exams, and any necessary screenings. Catching potential health problems early can make them easier to manage.

- **Self-Affirmation:** Believe in yourself and your capabilities. Affirm your worth, your skills, and your experience. Maintaining a positive self-view will help you overcome challenges and instill confidence in your colleagues and customers.

- **Time management:** Prioritize your tasks and responsibilities to ensure you have enough time for self-care activities. This may involve learning new time-management techniques or tools.

Now is the time for you to step forward with grace, confidence, and a bit of sass. You've got this!

Conclusion

Case Study: Mary

In this case study, we will explore the inspiring journey of Mary Thompson, a woman in her 60s who successfully overcame ageism, sexism, and other challenges to pursue her dream of becoming a therapist specializing in helping seniors live fulfilling lives. Mary's story serves as a testament to her resilience, determination, and passion for making a positive impact on the lives of others.

Mary Thompson was born in a small town and raised in a conservative family. Despite her intellectual curiosity and a deep interest in psychology, societal expectations at the time limited her educational opportunities. Mary got married at a young age and dedicated herself to raising her children and supporting her husband's career. However, after her children had grown up and she entered her 60s, Mary found herself yearning for a new purpose and the chance to pursue her lifelong dream.

Mary encountered societal stereotypes suggesting that older individuals were less capable of learning or starting new careers. Similarly, she faced gender-based discrimination, which assumed that women's professional aspirations diminished with age.

Despite these challenges, Mary had an unwavering belief in her abilities. She recognized that her life experiences and empathetic nature were valuable assets that would enrich her journey in psychology. With the support of her loved ones and her own determination, Mary decided to break through these barriers and follow her passion.

Mary began by conducting extensive research on psychology programs, seeking institutions that were inclusive, accommodating, and supportive of non-traditional students. She enrolled in a local university that offered flexible schedules and tailored support services.

Returning to school was not without its difficulties. Mary had to juggle family commitments, part-time work, and coursework. However, her strong time-management skills, discipline, and unwavering motivation helped her overcome these challenges.

Mary recognized the need to refresh her academic skills and familiarize herself with the latest developments in psychology. She sought assistance from professors, joined study groups, and engaged in independent research to bridge the knowledge gap.

Despite being older than her classmates, Mary embraced the opportunity to learn from individuals with diverse perspectives and life experiences. She actively participated in class discussions, offering unique insights and fostering meaningful interactions.

During her studies, Mary discovered a deep interest in geriatric psychology. She recognized the pressing need for specialized mental health support for seniors and was determined to contribute to this field.

Mary pursued additional coursework and practical experience in geriatric psychology. She interned at local senior care facilities and participated in research projects focused on aging-related issues, further enhancing her expertise.

Upon earning her degree, Mary embarked on establishing her own therapy practice, specializing in helping seniors live full lives. She created a safe and empathetic environment where older individuals could address emotional and psychological challenges unique to their age group.

Mary's empathetic approach and extensive knowledge in geriatric psychology have positively impacted the lives of numerous seniors. Through individual therapy sessions, support groups, and educational workshops, Mary helps her clients embrace aging, navigate transitions, and find fulfillment in their later years.

Mary actively engages with the local community, organizing events, and collaborating with organizations that promote senior well-being. She speaks at conferences, writes articles, and advocates for policies that address ageism and support the mental health needs of older adults.

Mary's dedication and contributions have garnered recognition within her field. She has received accolades for her pioneering work in geriatric psychology and has been invited to share her experiences and expertise on various media platforms.

Mary Thompson's story exemplifies the power of determination, resilience, and a genuine desire to make a difference. Overcoming ageism, sexism, and societal expectations, Mary pursued her dream of becoming a therapist specializing in helping seniors live fulfilling lives. Through her compassion, knowledge, and unwavering commitment, she has transformed the lives of countless individuals, challenging stereotypes and inspiring others to embrace their passions at any age. Mary's journey serves as an inspiration for people of all generations, highlighting the importance of pursuing one's dreams and breaking through societal barriers.

The End...

As I sit here, penning the final words of this remarkable journey we've embarked on together, I am overwhelmed with a profound sense of gratitude. Thank you for accompanying me through the pages of *Women Starting Over at 60*, a heartfelt guide designed to uplift, support, and inspire women who find themselves at a pivotal crossroads in life. It has been an honor to share this transformative experience with you.

Throughout this book, we have explored the vast possibilities that lie ahead for women over 60. We have jumped into the depths of your fears, dreams, and desires, recognizing that age is merely a number and that the power to reinvent oneself knows no bounds.

Together, we have dismantled societal expectations and shattered the barriers that society often places upon us as we age.

In every chapter, I have sought to offer you not only practical advice, tips, and strategies, but also a gentle reminder of your inherent worth and resilience. Your age does not diminish your significance in today's society; on the contrary, it is the culmination of a life rich with experiences, wisdom, and the potential for infinite possibilities.

In sharing the inspiring stories and remarkable case studies of women who have triumphed over adversity, we have witnessed the indomitable spirit that resides within each and every one of us. These stories serve as a testament to the fact that it is never too late to pursue your passions, fulfill your dreams, and make a lasting impact on the world.

My intention has always been to empower you—to ignite a fire within your soul and remind you of the tremendous power that lies dormant, waiting to be awakened. I hope you have felt the warmth of encouragement, support, and unwavering belief in your potential radiating from these pages. And as you close the final chapter, I implore you to carry that flame with you, nurturing it and allowing it to guide you on your unique journey.

Please know that your presence on this expedition has been immeasurably valuable. The stories you've shared, the challenges you've faced, and the triumphs you've celebrated have enriched the tapestry of this book. Your courage to start anew, to embrace change, and to believe in your own abilities serves as an inspiration not only to me but to countless others who may stumble upon these words.

As we part ways, I would be remiss if I did not humbly ask for a small favor. If *Women Starting Over at 60* has touched your heart, ignited a spark within your spirit, or provided you with even a glimmer of hope and encouragement, I kindly request that you consider leaving a review on Amazon. Your review will not only help other women discover this empowering guide but also serve as a testament to the strength and resilience of women over 60.

In conclusion, I want to assure you that this is not the end, but rather the beginning of an extraordinary chapter in your life. You are embarking on a journey of self-discovery, growth, and limitless potential. Embrace the challenges that come your way, for they are opportunities in disguise.

Thank you once again for joining me on this remarkable odyssey. It has been an absolute joy to guide you through the pages of this book. May your days be filled with boundless joy, endless possibilities, and an unwavering belief in your own power and worth.

With heartfelt gratitude,

GiGi K

Resources

1. Government websites such as the Bureau of Labor Statistics (BLS) and the US Department of Labor offer data and information on employment trends, career outlooks, and job opportunities.

2. Professional organizations such as the National Association of Career Development (NACD) and the National Career Development Association (NCDA) provide resources and support for career changers and job seekers.

3. Non-profit organizations such as AARP, which offer resources and information on employment and job training programs for older workers. https://www.aarp.org/work/job-search/

4. Online career resources such as LinkedIn, Indeed, and Glassdoor provide job listings and career advice.

5. Academic journals and publications, such as the Journal of Career Development and Career Development Quarterly, offer research and insights on career development and job market trends.

6. Books and e-books on career changes and career development, including bestsellers like

What Color is Your Parachute? by Richard Bolles and *The 50+ Career Change* by Marci Alboher.

7. Websites and blogs specializing in career change, such as CareerChange.net, CareerPivot.com, and SecondCareers.com offer tips, advice, and resources for older workers making a career transition.

8. Professional career coaches and trainers, who offer personalized guidance and support for career changers.

9. Local community colleges and adult education programs, which offer courses and training programs to help individuals acquire new skills and change careers.

10. Online learning platforms like Coursera, Udemy, and edX, which offer courses and certifications in various industries and skills, making it easier for individuals to learn new skills and transition into new careers. (Note that Udemy has courses on changing careers and finding your purpose).

11. https://encorenetwork.org/

12. Clearerthinking.org

References

Alan. (2021, November 26). *Starting over at 60 with nothing. How to turn your finances around at 60.»* financial planning. Financiallyhappy. ltd. https://financiallyhappy.ltd/starting-over-at-60-with-nothing/

Bolton, D. (2023, March 14). *Obstacles that the elderly face when working.* Retire Fearless. https://www.retirefearless.com/post/obstacles-that-the-elderly-face-when-working

Boothe, G. (2022, August 3). *The 9 best businesses to start over 60.* Entrepreneur. https://www.entrepreneur.com/finance/the-9-best-businesses-to-start-over-60/432661

Brett Stumm. (2022, August 31). *How to find your passion and purpose in life after 60* - brett stumm. https://brettstumm.com/finding-purpose-in-life-after-60/

Brubaker, M. (2020, January 10). *Lonely in a crowd: Overcoming loneliness with acceptance and wisdom: Study looked at characteristics of loneliness in a senior housing community and the strategies residents used to overcome it.* ScienceDaily. https://www.sciencedaily.com/releases/2020/01/200110101033.htm

Carpenter, W. (2021). *Challenges older women face re-entering the workforce: Expanding after career opportunities.* https://research.library.mun.ca/15268/1/thesis.pdf

Center on Budget and Policy Priorities. (2020, August 13). *Policy basics: Top ten facts about social security.* Center on Budget and Policy Priorities. https://www.cbpp.org/research/social-security/top-ten-facts-about-social-security

Cocozza, P. (2022a, July 25). *A new start after 60: "I didn't want to be an invisible old lady – so I became a yoga teacher."* The Guardian. https://www.theguardian.com/lifeandstyle/2022/jul/25/a-new-start-after-60-i-didnt-want-to-be-an-invisible-old-lady-so-i-became-a-yoga-teacher

Cocozza, P. (2022b, August 29). *A new start after 60: "I've finally become the artist I always felt I was inside."* The Guardian. https://www.theguardian.com/lifeandstyle/2022/aug/29/a-new-start-after-60-ive-finally-become-the-artist-i-always-felt-i-was-inside

Cocozza, P. (2023, March 6). *A new start after 60: I retired – and began to follow my dreams.* The Guardian. https://www.theguardian.com/lifeandstyle/2023/mar/06/a-new-start-after-60-i-retired-and-began-to-follow-my-dreams

Coxwell, K. (2020, July 2). *The pros and cons of returning to work after retirement.* NewRetirement. https://www.newretirement.com/retirement/g

oing-back-to-work-after-retirement-the-good-
the-bad-and-the-ugly/

E. Budson, A. (2021, September 16). *Can physical or cognitive activity prevent dementia?* Harvard Health. https://www.health.harvard.edu/blog/can-physical-or-cognitive-activity-prevent-dementia-202109162595

Filges, T., Siren, A., Friedberg, T., & Nielsen, B. C. V. (2020). Voluntary work for the physical and mental health of older volunteers: A systematic review. *Campbell Systematic Reviews, 16(4), 1.* https://doi.org/10.1002/cl2.1124

Fontinelle, A. (2021, May 27). *Pink tax.* Investopedia. https://www.investopedia.com/pink-tax-5095458

Gerhardt, M. W., Nachemson-Ekwall, J., & Fogel, B. (2022, March 8). *Harnessing the power of age diversity.* Harvard Business Review. https://hbr.org/2022/03/harnessing-the-power-of-age-diversity

Godlove, A. (2022, September 9). *4 things I wish I would have known before retiring abroad.* TravelAwaits. https://www.travelawaits.com/2801158/retirement-diaries-panama-retirement-lifestyle-coach/

Gordon, M. (2019, May 25). *What's your purpose? Finding a sense of meaning in life is linked to health.* NPR. https://www.npr.org/sections/health-shots/2019/05/25/726695968/whats-your-

purpose-finding-a-sense-of-meaning-in-life-is-
linked-to-health?utm_id=7598562&orgid=

Hegg, J. (2017). *110 activities for the elderly & seniors
[ultimate list]*. In vivehealth.com.
https://www.vivehealth.com/blogs/resources/
activities-elderly-seniors

Ibarra, H., Ely, R., & Kolb, D. (2013, September).
Women rising: The unseen barriers. Harvard
Business Review.
https://hbr.org/2013/09/women-rising-the-
unseen-barriers

Indeed. (2022, December 9). *How to change your career
after 60.* Indeed.
https://www.indeed.com/career-
advice/starting-new-job/changing-career-at-60

International Churchill Society. (n.d.). *Quotes archives.*
International Churchill Society. Retrieved June
10, 2023, from
https://winstonchurchill.org/resources/quotes
/?gclid=CjwKCAjwvpCkBhB4EiwAujULMkg
WEIPopyXvQia-
uo6NxMpOA2KNMJFeVkGrEHHjiFwljo4ZW
15yDRoCIJUQAvD_BwE

IRS. (2019, June 4). *Topic no. 751 social security and
Medicare withholding rate.* Www.irs.gov.
https://www.irs.gov/taxtopics/tc751#:~:text=
The%20current%20tax%20rate%20for

Lee, J. (2021, December 12). *"Money is running out":
Financial stress drives retirees back to work.* NBC

News. https://www.nbcnews.com/news/us-news/money-running-out-financial-stress-drives-retirees-back-work-n1285736

Leveraging the value of an age-diverse workforce. (n.d.). SHRM Foundation. https://www.shrm.org/foundation/ourwork/in itiatives/the-aging-workforce/Documents/Age Divers-Workforce-Executive-Briefing.pdf

Loney, S. (2023, March 8). *Diminished. devalued. demeaned. Ageism is pushing women out of work – and they're over it.* Thestar.com. https://www.thestar.com/life/2023/women-work-ageism.html

Manning, M. (2019a, March 4). *6 strategies to help you get the most from life after 60.* Sixty and Me. https://sixtyandme.com/6-strategies-to-help-you-get-the-most-from-life-after-60/

Manning, M. (2019b, August 30). *6 ways to find lasting happiness after 60.* Fashion, Hair, Makeup for Older Women, Senior Dating, Travel. https://sixtyandme.com/6-simple-ways-to-stay-happy-and-positive-after-50/

Marte, J. (2017, June 2). *5 common financial struggles faced by people over 60.* Washington Post. https://www.washingtonpost.com/news/get-there/wp/2017/06/02/5-financial-struggles-seniors-face-that-go-beyond-retirement/

Mercado, D. (2019, July 18). *Retiring this year? How much you'll need for healthcare costs.* CNBC.

---

https://www.cnbc.com/2019/07/18/retiring-this-year-how-much-youll-need-for-health-care-costs.html

Mikhail, A. (2023, February 1). *"Am I useless now?" Aging women in the workforce face a crisis of confidence and experts say they simply deserve more.* Fortune Well. https://fortune.com/well/2023/02/01/aging-women-in-the-workforce-face-a-crisis-of-confidence/

Morrow-Howell, N. (2015). *The financial vulnerability of older adults.* Institute for Public Health. https://publichealth.wustl.edu/the-financial-vulnerability-of-older-adults/

Overcoming your 5 biggest retirement challenges. (2022, August). Morgan Stanley. https://www.morganstanley.com/articles/retirement-challenges

Pelta, R. (2019, December 14). *Generational communication gaps aren't about age.* FlexJobs. https://www.flexjobs.com/blog/post/workplace-generational-communication-gaps/

Peters, E. (2021, January 29). *Why you need A midlife mentor.* Making Midlife Matter. https://makingmidlifematter.com/why-you-need-midlife-mentor/

Policy basics: Top ten facts about social security. (2020, August 13). *Center on Budget and Policy Priorities.* https://www.cbpp.org/research/social-security/top-ten-facts-about-social-security

Prvulovic, T. (2022, January 28). *Finding your passions in retirement-5 steps.* Second Wind Movement. https://secondwindmovement.com/finding-passions/

Rampton, J. (2016, May 24). *15 steps I took to successfully reinvent myself after losing everything.* Entrepreneur. https://www.entrepreneur.com/growing-a-business/15-steps-i-took-to-successfully-reinvent-myself-after/276263

Robinson, L., & Segal, J. (2019, March 28). *Volunteering and its surprising benefits.* HelpGuide.org. https://www.helpguide.org/articles/healthy-living/volunteering-and-its-surprising-benefits.htm

Ruth, A. (2015, July 31). *Winston Churchill – We make a life by what we give.* Due. https://due.com/winston-churchill-we-make-a-life-by-what-we-give/

Senior Lifestyle. (2022, January 6). *How to make new friends after 60.* Senior Lifestyle. https://www.seniorlifestyle.com/resources/blog/how-to-make-new-friends-after-60/

Shift. (2019, June 28). *How to find your passion after retirement.* Shift. https://www.shift.is/2019/06/how-to-find-your-passion-after-retirement/

Shockley, M. M. (2022, December 25). *10 inspiring retirement stories you'll love from 2022.* TravelAwaits.

https://www.travelawaits.com/2843332/best-retirement-stories-2022/

Stanley, M. (2022, August 24). *Overcoming your 5 biggest retirement challenges.* Morgan Stanley. https://www.morganstanley.com/articles/retire ment-challenges

Steptoe, A., & Fancourt, D. (2019). Leading a meaningful life at older ages and its relationship with social engagement, prosperity, health, biology, and time use. *Proceedings of the National Academy of Sciences, 116(4), 1207–1212.* https://doi.org/10.1073/pnas.1814723116

Study: Volunteering is good for your health. (2020, June 16). *Harvard School of Public Health.* https://www.hsph.harvard.edu/news/hsph-in-the-news/study-volunteering-is-good-for-your-health/

Stumm, B. (2022, July 27). *Finding your passion after retirement: Happy retirement tip.* Brett Stumm. https://brettstumm.com/finding-your-passion-after-retirement/

Sullivan, M. (2017, December 6). *Take charge America helps consumers tackle financial new year's resolutions.* Www.businesswire.com. https://www.businesswire.com/news/home/2 0171206005253/en/Take-Charge-America-Helps-Consumers-Tackle-Financial-New-Year%E2%80%99s-Resolutions

Taking Care. (2022, April 7). *10 of the most beneficial hobbies and interests for the over 60s.* PPP Taking Care. https://taking.care/blogs/resources-advice/beneficial-hobbies-interests-for-over-60s

Turner, T. (2023, April 5). *Working after retirement.* RetireGuide. https://www.retireguide.com/retirement-life-leisure/working-after-retirement/

Waldman, E. (2021, August 31). How to manage a multi-generational team. Harvard Business Review. https://hbr.org/2021/08/how-to-manage-a-multi-generational-team

We make a living by what we get; we make a life by what we give. - Winston Churchill - Quotes Pedia. (n.d.). Quotespedia. https://www.quotespedia.org/authors/w/winston-churchill/we-make-a-living-by-what-we-get-we-make-a-life-by-what-we-give-winston-churchill/

Printed in Great Britain
by Amazon